GARLAND STUDIES ON

THE ELDERLY IN AMERICA

edited by

STUART BRUCHEY
ALLAN NEVINS PROFESSOR EMERITUS
COLUMBIA UNIVERSITY

A GARLAND SERIES

CAREGIVING DAUGHTERS

ACCEPTING THE ROLE OF CAREGIVER FOR ELDERLY PARENTS

RICK BRIGGS

GARLAND PUBLISHING, INC.
A MEMBER OF THE TAYLOR & FRANCIS GROUP
NEW YORK & LONDON / 1998

Library of Congress Cataloging-in-Publication Data

Briggs, Rick, 1945–
    Caregiving daughters : accepting the role of caregiver for
elderly parents / Rick Briggs.
        p.   cm. — (Garland studies on the elderly in America)
    Includes bibliographical references and index.
    ISBN 0-8153-3027-8 (alk. paper)
    1. Aging parents—Care—United States. 2. Daughters—
United States—Family relationships—Interviews. 3. Adult children—United States—Family relationships—Interviews.
4. Caregivers—United States—Family relationships—Interviews.
I. Title. II. Series.
HQ1064.U5B75 1997
306.874—dc21   97-35312

Printed on acid-free, 250-year-life paper
Manufactured in the United States of America

Dedicated to
those who provide
care and caring for our elders

Contents

List of Tables

Preface

There is an enduring legend concerning the old in many Asian countries. The legend varies somewhat from one culture to the next, but a persisting theme runs through these ancient stories. At a particular point in the lives of the community's elders—at a time when they are no longer so productive, when they consume more than they contribute, when their continued existence threatens the survival of the struggling community—they are carried on the backs of their sons to a far and high mountain and abandoned.

In some legends the old die there; in others, their sons, their families, or the community reconsider and rush to preserve what they come to realize is a valuable resource. In certain legends the elders become heroes and, through their wisdom, rescue the younger people from impending doom. It seems ironic that this portrayal of abandonment is so pervasive in a part of the world that, in the eyes of Westerners, reveres their old and cares deeply for elders in the family.

We are not without our own fables and legends in America. We steadfastly hold to our own myth of neglect. Comparing today to yesteryear, we measure ourselves with the yardstick of nostalgia and come up short. We have come to believe as fact the notion that, until modern times, families flawlessly provided for, nurtured and cared for their older members. Elders were loved, valued and esteemed. Three generations lived under one roof in near perfect harmony. Somehow, the story goes, in recent times we have lost that idyllic way of life. With our twentieth century focus on youth, we fail to prize the rich resource that we have in the older generation. We neglect and abandon our old.

While there is a kernel of truth in most legends, there is probably not much factual basis to either of these. Neither Americans nor Asians are turning their backs on their old. These stories are not meant to be reports of actual happenings. Rather, their value lies in the reminder that they provide us, the caution—lest we forget.

We are accountable—we, as a society, and we, as individuals. We have a responsibility to our old—though not to the exclusion of our immediate family, our community, and ourselves. These and other obligations of life must be delicately balanced. They will not all receive equal time and attention, but none should exact so much from us that it tips us completely in one direction or the other.

That balancing act is becoming more and more of a Herculean feat. The pool of young and middle-aged will soon begin to shrink, while the cohort of elders grows exponentially. The alarm has been sounded. The elderly are coming! An avalanche if by land, a tidal wave if by sea. We may not be prepared, but we are undeniably forewarned. This is no sneak attack.

Whether or not a workable system is put in place by the time the baby boomers reach late life—stating their needs and asserting their rights—this present generation of elders and their adult children are left, by and large, to wrestle with this question of filial responsibility and to face the challenges on their own. And while most older adults desire, above all else, to live out their lives without becoming a burden to their children, the sad reality is that most will not navigate the sometimes treacherous waters of later life without some help. Independence, as an ideal, gives way to the more realistic idea of interdependence as a way of life. As years go by, the scales tip more and more toward dependence. And while at-risk elders may initially attempt to get their needs met via formal assistance from public and private service programs, they turn inevitably to the family for help that is difficult to get from strangers.

And families respond. Most do this willingly, without asking whether they ought to or whether they have to. They do it without question. One day the adult daughter is an accountant, and the next, she is a caregiver. One day the adult son is a mechanic and his wife runs a small business, and the next, they are caregivers. They come to this role with no training, little or no information, and no psychological preparation. More often than not, there is no transition time. They frequently live in geographic areas where there is a scarcity of services available. Where services do exist, families who suddenly find themselves in the caregiving role have little knowledge of them and less understanding of how to access them or make use of their services.

Since family members are not paid caregivers, they are, by definition volunteers—regardless of the level of enthusiasm with which they agreed to take on the task. Unlike the many good and kind souls who are agency volunteers, giving several hours of their time each day to keep myriad social and health service organizations alive and well in times of scarce resources, these family volunteers will, more likely than not, commit to twenty-four hours a day, 365 days a year. Unlike their agency counterparts, they will not receive gold plaques or appreciation awards. They will not be honored at recognition dinners. They will silently give up a non-refundable portion of their lives and make a daily sacrifice that will go largely unnoticed by the rest of society. They will give of themselves to meet the physical and health, social, psychological, financial, and spiritual needs of their aging parents.

They will do this whether they are naturally good at it or not, for the desire to care is not the same as ability to care, and little assistance is available to help caregivers grow and develop in their role. This lack of support is due, in part, to policy makers and politicians who, faced with dwindling coffers and opinion polls that warn against increased taxation, would like to divorce themselves from any responsibility for grappling with this problem and simply shift responsibility to the family.

But this does not have to be an either-or proposition. It does not have to be all or nothing. If the issue of care of our elderly is ever to be truly addressed, it will come about as a result of a sense of shared responsibility. Families need assistance from private and public service agencies, and the formal aging network needs the support of families.

This idea of shared responsibility is a new thought for us to consider. Indeed, care of the elderly is an issue that requires new thinking. Old ways do not always solve new problems. And this is a new problem, if not by its nature, at least in scope.

There is no denying that, throughout history, many individual families have provided care for their elderly. Yet, this is not an issue that has been dealt with on a grand scale by previous generations. A life expectancy of forty-seven years at the beginning of the twentieth century suggests that, while not necessarily uncommon, the need for the role of caring for elderly family members was not nearly so pervasive as it is today. This is no longer an individual family problem.

Today, this is a complex societal issue. It is not one for which we presently have an answer. It is a problem that can only be understood slowly, over time. It is comprised of layers. Peel one off to examine it, and another is exposed—a deeper layer, requiring a deeper level of understanding.

Where do we begin in this journey toward understanding? A starting point would seem to be in trying to gain some knowledge of the one group providing the bulk of care—adult daughters. Who are these women? The label 'family caregiver' disguises them and conceals them from our view. We need to look beyond the label. It is said that by focusing so intently on details that we sometimes overlook the big picture. We can't see the forest for the trees. In this case, we may be seeing the forest, but failing to consider the individual trees—the real live individual human beings who make up this large anonymous group that we call caregivers.

This generation of daughters did not know that they would become the trailblazers for a society exploring the new territory of extended life. Today, we hear little girls dream of things that previous generations never could have imagined. They dream of becoming dancers and doctors, scientists and senators. Few probably dream of one day becoming a caregiver. Yet, that is precisely the reality of many of today's adult daughters. How did this come about? What led them to this role? To understand this is to begin to know something about their experience. And to understand daughters who care is to take the first step in providing the help that they need and deserve.

Acknowledgments

I would like to express my appreciation to Ardeth Deay, chair of my research committee, for the encouragement, guidance, and occasional prodding that she gave me during this project. The personal and philosophical discussions that we held over the course of time came to mean more to me than the technical assistance that I needed to complete this study.

My committee members have been an invaluable resource for me. They have my gratitude for their assistance and support throughout this endeavor. I want to thank Jody Wolfe and Mona Counts for encouraging me to venture into the virgin territory of qualitative research and for giving me direction and assurance when I was bewildered at times. I want to express my thanks to Perry Phillips for providing me a second chance to accomplish this task and for being a steady rock to lean on. My thanks also go to Barbara Judy for the confidence that she continually instills in me. Joy Saab came to my aid at the critical close of this project and agreed to take on a responsibility that was in no way required or expected of her. I appreciate that act of kindness. I would also like to express my gratitude to Craig Johnson for the technical and emotional support that he provided during the final stage of preparation of this manuscript.

I am grateful beyond words to the adult daughters in this study who gave me their time, shared with me their lives and their thoughts, and explored with me family histories which were sometimes difficult for me to understand and painful for them to discuss. I find them nothing short of heroes for the sacrifices that they have made, the care that they have given, and their willingness to open up their lives so that others may learn.

Finally, I want to give my thanks and my love to my wife, Paula, my daughters, Lisa and Amanda, and my parents, Donald and Evelyn, for believing in me.

Caregiving Daughters

CHAPTER I

Introduction

Perhaps dementia has always been with us. It receives more attention today than it did a few short decades ago because of improved diagnostic procedures and increased coverage by the news media. But beyond these factors is a more important reason for the notice it presently receives. The number of cases of dementia has increased dramatically throughout this century and is expected to continue well into the next.

The cause of this increase can be found in a demographic picture of the United States. While dementia can strike the young and middle-aged as well as the elderly, it is far more common in the old. At the turn of the century there were just over 3 million individuals aged 65 and older in the nation. Today, there are ten times that many elders. The life expectancy of 47 years in 1900 fits better with the concept of middle-age today (Fradkin & Heath, 1992). What these demographic changes mean is that more Americans are living to an age where they have the dubious opportunity to develop dementia.

It is likely that as long as dementia has been in existence, caregivers of cognitively-impaired individuals have supported them. Today's caregivers, however, are different in some ways from their predecessors. Their numbers are greater, the environment for care and competing demands are different, and the role is longer in duration.

This present generation is really the first to experience caregiving on this grand scale. They are, in a sense, pioneers. And just like their ancestors who came to this country, they must endure hardships and explore unknown territory. They must possess the determination and courage that enable them to continue on without the benefit of a road map. And while they struggle to form connections with each other and those who can help, they must ultimately face much of this struggle alone.

These pioneering caregivers are the focus of this book. They need help and support. A starting place is to learn as much as possible about them and their role. While a great deal of information has been gathered over the past decade, there is a shortage of data in some areas.

STATEMENT OF THE PROBLEM

The role of women as caregivers has been well documented in the literature (Guberman, Maheu, & Maille, 1992). The literature confirms her place in caregiving and describes just how she provides that care. Less attention has been given to why she is the caregiver. To some extent, it has been accepted as a natural course of events. Women have always been caregivers. That has been their historical role. First with babies, then with children, later with their spouses' parents, (recently, in the work place), and finally with their husbands, women have been caregivers across the life span.

But, does it necessarily follow that caring for babies automatically compels a woman to take on the role of caregiver of infirm elderly? There is an assumption that it is the natural way of things. If she is not always eager to accept the role, she is, at least willing. And demographics of caregiving seem to bear out that supposition.

What is the process by which this takes place? What societal and personal factors are at play? What subtle and not so subtle pressures influence her selection? If gender differences in life expectancy provide part of the answer for elderly wives, the predicament of middle-aged daughters remains somewhat a mystery. The problem is, quite simply, little is known about how daughters find themselves in this almost inevitable position, to the near exclusion of their brothers.

PURPOSE OF THE STUDY

The purpose of this study is to identify factors that influence the selection of adult daughters as primary caregivers for their older parents. Further, the intent is to fully describe those factors and the process by which the daughters consciously or unconsciously chose the role or were assigned the role of family caregiver.

The circumstances that were present throughout the process will be explored. The full implications of the context in which the decision was made to assume the care of the impaired elderly family member will be considered.

RESEARCH QUESTION

This study is an attempt to answer the following question: What factors influence the selection of adult daughters as primary caregivers of parents with dementia? To fully explore that question the examination will have to go beyond the expected answers of love and family responsibility. For while they may be, in part, an explanation for why families provide care, they fail to explain how it is that daughters specifically end up so often in that role. Taking that one step further, how is it that one particular daughter, in a family with more than one available, is chosen for the role?

IMPORTANCE OF THE RESEARCH QUESTION

One of the dangers of a narrowly focused research question is that, even after the answer is discovered, no one cares. The researcher is faced with the proverbial, "So what?"

While this study is only a first step in the understanding of a very complex issue, there is value in its findings and in the results of related studies that will follow. It is a question that needs an answer.

No one who works in a helping profession with older adults denies the importance of understanding the family dynamics involved. One seldom works with an older adult in isolation. The "client" most often becomes the family unit. Anything that can be learned about the family and its interrelationships, then, is valuable.

The primary benefactor of this study, however, is the caregiver. If society is to finally provide much needed help to those who care for elderly family members, we need to know not only what information, skills and coping strategies they can be taught, but also how to motivate and encourage them. The first of these lessen caregiver burden; the latter provide positive reinforcement. It is difficult to know how to motivate caregivers to continue providing quality care unless there is some understanding of their original motivation.

Understanding factors leading to their role as caregivers can also help professionals appreciate some of the stress that caregivers presently experience. It can identify possible "pay-offs" for caregivers.

It can help explain some behaviors of caregivers that are difficult to understand (e.g., why some cannot ask for help, why others say that they do not want help). Findings in the study might point to personality characteristics such as non-assertiveness, which could put the caregiver at risk.

On the other hand, the results might illustrate satisfactions inherent in the caregiving role. That could lead to a better understanding of why some receive a sense of pleasure and fulfillment from the role and others do not. Even though the caregiving role is a heavy role, it might be possible to offset some of that weight by encouraging a more balanced perspective.

Most important, however, is that by understanding the factors that so often lead to the daughter's selection as caregiver, it may be possible to help her consciously decide whether to accept that role or not. In the process, the other family members might be forced to deal with the unfairness of the role of lone caregiver. On a broader scale, society at large may see the gross inequity of the gender-based role designation imposed upon this generation of women and decide to do better by those to follow.

CHAPTER II

Review of Literature

While caregivers who provide assistance to family members with disabling conditions as different as cancer, congestive heart disease, and cognitive decline may share some common characteristics and experiences, the focus of this book is exclusively on family caregivers of individuals with dementia. Providing a review of existing literature, this chapter contains (a) a definition and description of the dementias, (b) a portrait of the family caregiver, and (c) an explanation of the education needs of those providing care.

The aim of the chapter is to provide a context in which to understand one specific type of caregiver: the adult daughter of a parent with senile dementia. It is this most burdened, little researched and least supported family member who will be the focus of this research study.

DEMENTIA

Definition

The term *dementia* is a rather broad and somewhat vague term that, in the minds of some, lacks the clarity necessary for shared understanding among researchers and clinicians (Edwards, 1993; Maletta, 1990). The literal meaning of the Latin word *demens* is to be out of one's mind. In the late nineteenth century it was synonymous with insanity and was used to describe all mental disease; over the years it has been in and out of favor as a diagnostic term (Wang, 1977). As knowledge and understanding of disorders producing intellectual deterioration has increased, the term has undergone an evolution in definition. While imperfect, it is an improvement over earlier medical terms such as *organic brain syndrome* (Cummings & Benson, 1983) and the non-medical, popular term *senility*.

While not strictly a definition, perhaps the most reliable source for the meaning of dementia is found in the criteria developed by the American Psychiatric Association for the *Diagnostic and Statistical Manual of Mental Disorders*. In its most recent revision (*DSM-IV*), the following diagnostic criteria are listed:

1. Evidence of impaired memory (both new and previously learned information).
2. Evidence of at least one of the following cognitive disturbances:
   A. Language disturbances (aphasia).
   B. Impairment in motor ability, despite intact motor function (apraxia).
   C. Inability to recognize or identify objects, despite normal sensory function (agnosia).
   D. Difficulties in planning, organizing and sequencing. as well as abstract thinking.
3. Evidence that 1 and 2 interfere with work or social functioning to a significant extent and represent a significant decline from a previous level of functioning.
4. Assurance that these behaviors do not occur solely during the course of Delirium (American Psychiatric Association, 1994).

Types of Dementia

Historically, two broad categories of dementia have been identified (presenile and senile), with the arbitrary chronological age of 65 being the line of demarcation. There is need of further designation of type for the sake of clarity in clinical or research work. Whitehouse (1993) includes five broad types in his treatment of the subject.

Degenerative Dementias

The degenerative dementias are diseases of unknown etiology that are marked by a gradually progressive disintegration of the central nervous system. This disintegration appears to be related to the aging of the organism (Civil, Whitehouse, Lanska, & Mayeux, 1993). This category includes Alzheimer's Disease, Pick's Disease, Huntington's Disease and Parkinson's Disease, among others.

Vascular Dementias

Multi-infarct dementia is second only to Alzheimer's Disease in occurrence of cognitive disorders among the elderly. It is the most common of the vascular dementias (Marshall, 1993). Multi-infarct dementia refers to a series of slight strokes. A blood clot, air bubble, or other particle obstructs the circulatory system, blocking blood flow to the brain and resulting in the death of brain tissue (Edwards, 1993). With enough neurons destroyed in certain parts of the brain, dementia will result.

Viral Dementias

Less common than the first two types are the viral dementias, caused by a viral infection that affects the central nervous system. Until recently, probably the best known of these diseases was Creutzfeldt-Jakob Disease. The disease, resulting from a slow-growing virus, has been recognized since 1920 (Edwards, 1993). It is relatively rare, with an incidence of only one per million population per year (McArthur, Roos, & Johnson, 1993).

The most recently described viral dementia is human immunodeficiency virus (HIV) encephalopathy (McArthur, Roos, & Johnson, 1993). It is likely to quickly eclipse all other viral dementias in notoriety.

Bacterial, Fungal, and Parasitic Causes of Dementia

In this type of dementia the membranes surrounding the brain and spinal cord are infected, resulting in meningitis. Before antibiotics only about 5% of individuals with meningitis survived; the survival rate is now 95%. However, 85% of elderly survivors are left with neurologic complications. Still, only about 1% of all cases of dementia are the result of central nervous system infection (Ashe, Rosen, McArthur, & Davis, 1993).

Metabolic Dementia

Metabolic disorders produce widespread changes in the biochemistry and physiology of the brain. The cause can be from a system deficiency or an assault from some external toxin. The most common of these disturbances is the result of the ingestion of medication (Feldman & Plum, 1993). The damage may be caused by an idiosyncratic susceptibility of a particular individual to a certain medication, or it may be caused by medication overdose or the negative interaction of two drugs.

Other common external agents include alcohol, carbon monoxide, DDT, and lead. Dementia can also result from dysfunction of the endocrine system, such as hypothyroidism, cardiovascular and pulmonary failure, and nutritional deficiencies (Feldman & Plum, 1993).

Miscellaneous Causes of Dementia

A catch-all group is added to include those causes that do not fall into one of the above categories. Those causes include hydrocephalus, trauma, neoplasia (tumors), multiple sclerosis, and epilepsy.

Other Classification Systems

The five types of dementia delineated by Whitehouse are not the only types of dementia recognized. Specific disorders within the five categories have been organized under different headings by other authors, and different classifications have been used for different purposes. For instance, Heston (1983) divides the dementing illnesses into three groups: primary undifferentiated dementia, primary differentiated dementia, and secondary dementia.

While an exhaustive listing of various classifications is unnecessary, two additional methods of differentiation might be useful. The first is that of classifying the dementias as either reversible or irreversible. The term *reversible* implies the possibility of medical intervention that could lead to the cognitive impairment being checked or even eliminated. At present, neurological diseases (e.g., Alzheimer's, Creutzfeldt-Jacob, Pick's, Huntington's, normal pressure hydrocephalus) would be classified as irreversible, while depression, infection, dehydration, malnutrition, medication overdose, drug interactions, hormone imbalance, and vitamin deficiencies would be considered reversible (Sawyer, Ballard, & Autrey, 1990).

Another important distinction is that between dementia and pseudodementia, a term used for a disorder that can mimic dementing illnesses so closely that distinguishing between the two can require a good deal of expertise, experience and diagnostic rigor. Clearly, the most common of these is depression in the elderly (Emery, 1992). While young and middle-aged severely depressed individuals may exhibit some cognitive alterations, such as poor concentration and attention, they are unlikely to be diagnosed with dementia. Depressive dementia appears most often to fall in the domain of the elderly (Cummings & Benson, 1983).

Of course, it should be made clear that however these disorders are classified, an individual is not limited to one type of dementing illness. Having a cognitive disorder such as Alzheimer's Disease does not protect one from depression, stroke, or any of the other conditions previously mentioned.

Prevalence of Dementia

There is no clear evidence to demonstrate that there is, today, an increased incidence of dementia. Growing awareness of the magnitude of the problem over the last decade and a half probably relates more to extended life expectancy, improved diagnostic techniques and increased attention by the media. While there have been (and continue to be) many surveys of prevalence of dementia in the elderly, lack of uniformity in diagnostic criteria, use of different mechanisms of case identification, and differences in age distributions of populations studied have led to variability in prevalence estimates (Lanska & Schoenberg, 1993).

Estimates of dementia in the elderly range from 5% to 15% and higher. However, as Lanska and Schoenberg (1993) argue, comparing prevalence rates of "elderly" with dementia in two or more studies is meaningless. "The prevalence of severe dementia rises steeply from less than 1% at ages 65 to 70, to over 25% by age 85" (Lanska & Schoenberg, 1993, p. 17). The variation in age composition among the samples of "elderly" almost guarantees different results.

Senile Dementia of the Alzheimer's Type

Since dementia is a syndrome rather than a specific disease and encompasses a host of illnesses and disabling conditions, it might be useful to focus on one particular type of dementia and add specificity to the foregoing general description. In view of the fact that Alzheimer's Disease accounts for over half of all cases of dementia (Fraser, 1987), it seems the apparent choice for elaboration.

History

In 1906 a psychiatrist named Alois Alzheimer presented a paper to the Association of Southwest German Specialists in Mental Disorders that included what would become a classic case (Group for the Advancement of Psychiatry, 1988). While loss in memory and changes in personality had been reported by others in previous patient case reports, it was argued by Alzheimer that the degeneration of neurons and presence of "ganglion cells" in his relatively young patient demonstrated that this case represented a distinctive disease process (Benson, 1986). Alzheimer had, indeed, discovered a distinct disorder, but his focus on the young age of the patient inadvertently led to a delay of the massive research effort that was to come nearly 50 years later.

Alzheimer believed (as did most researchers who followed him) that senile dementia was caused by aging of the brain, and while it produced senile plaque in the brain, it failed to show evidence of the neurofibrillary tangles that had come to be one of the hallmarks of Alzheimer's Disease (Torack, 1981). Thus, in the minds of clinicians, the two conditions—senile dementia and Alzheimer's Disease—were two distinct entities. Senile dementia was thought to be an inevitable part of the aging process (Zarit, Orr, & Zarit, 1985). Alzheimer's Disease, on the other hand, was a true disease that affected relatively young people. Since the condition is relatively rare in young people (Lampe, 1987), the immensity of the problem went unrecognized (Benson, 1986). This faulty understanding persisted until 1968, when the syndrome was recognized as being the same regardless of the age of the individual (Torack, 1981). The result was a dramatic shift in perceived importance, as reflected in *Newsweek* labeling it "the disease of the century" (Clark, 1984).

Nature of the Disease

Most people associate memory problems with Alzheimer's Disease. This is understandable, since it is the hallmark of the disease and one of the earliest recognizable deficits. However, other traits need to be included for a fuller understanding of the disease.

Memory Impairment

Early in the disease victims forget names of acquaintances and terms used for everyday articles. They may become easily disoriented, getting lost in surroundings with which they are well-acquainted. This disorientation can occur in their neighborhood or yard, or in their own house or bedroom. This can result not only in confusion, but in a sense of panic as fear rises.

Simple tasks, such as keeping a check book or performing a routine, job-related activity, becomes overwhelming. Typically, recent memory is affected before long-term memory. Forgotten appointments and phone messages become too frequent to attribute to the normal benign forgetfulness that everyone experiences from time to time. As Mace and Rabins (1991, p. 28) so graphically describe the phenomenon, it is like forever "coming into the middle of a movie: one has no idea what happened just before what is happening now."

These memory problems develop slowly over time. It may be months or years before the individual, the family and others recognize a problem and seek help.

Judgment Problems

Forming a judgment requires individuals to gather pieces of information and mentally compare their relative value in reaching some conclusion or decision. This evaluative process and other forms of higher level, abstract thinking are beyond the capabilities of the Alzheimer's victim. This impairment in judgment could take the form of poor financial decisions, but it could just as well lead to problems of personal safety.

Driving a car, for instance, is a task so familiar to most people that they forget what a complex task it is. Of course, it requires great eye-hand-foot coordination; it requires memory, in terms of rules of the road, basic understanding of the physics of how an automobile functions, and steps required to operate the vehicle. But beyond this, safe operation of a car demands myriad judgments to be made with each trip.

Stopped at an intersection, drivers must judge the distance of vehicles approaching from either side. They must judge the speed with which those cars are approaching, as well as the distance across the intersection and the time required to travel that distance. Taking all of those things into account in a matter of seconds, they must make a judgment about the safety of crossing that intersection. While Alzheimer's victims are often unwilling to give up their right to drive, and families are reluctant to force the issue, it is far too complex a task for those with impaired judgment.

Language Difficulties

Aphasia, the loss of ability to use language, can begin rather innocuously, with simple speech hesitancy or minor difficulty in finding the right word. Alzheimer's victims might substitute a word that sounds similar (e.g., toe for tie, hand for hat) or they might substitute a related word or term (e.g., house for office, cutting thing for scissors). They may describe the object whose name they cannot recall: "it's that thing men wear around their neck".

Alzheimer's victims may produce what is referred to as word salad, stringing together phrases that seem to make sense, but leave the listener somewhat puzzled because the core message is missing. They may seem to be perfectly coherent in an initial conversation, but later discussions with them reveal that they have just a few stories which they repeat over and over.

This repetitious behavior can be seen in other instances, as well. A person may repeat the same word or the beginning of a word repetitively. The same question might be asked endlessly. This problem extends beyond language. It is not uncommon for individuals with Alzheimer's Disease to repeat physical actions unceasingly. They might fold and refold the laundry continually. They might pace about the living room incessantly in the same pattern. "It seems as if the damaged mind has a tendency to get stuck on one activity and has difficulty shifting gears to a new activity" (Mace & Rabins, 1991, p. 133).

Eventually the store of vocabulary shrinks, and they are reduced to phrases, single words, and unintelligible muttering or shrieks. They may be mute in the last stage of the disease.

Alzheimer's victims have as much difficulty in receiving communication as they do in transmitting it. Victims may need instructions broken down into the simplest commands. Information might need to be repeated slowly to be understood. Failure in communication can lead to great frustration on the part of victim and caregiver alike.

Recognition Problems

Recognition of words is not the only identification problem of Alzheimer's patients. They might just as easily fail to recognize what an everyday object is used for. Such a person might try to shave with a hairbrush. They will eventually also have difficulty in identifying persons with whom they are well-acquainted. Even a son, daughter, spouse or other caregiver can become a total stranger to the individual with Alzheimer's Disease.

Loss of Sense of Time

Time is extremely important in American society. Even without access to a watch or clock, most people are amazingly good at judging the passage of time. Alzheimer's victims may retain the feeling of importance of time, but lose the ability to interpret it. This may cause the individual to become agitated and continually ask what time it is. Patients may be able to read a clock or calendar in the early stages, but have little understanding of what it means. Does two o'clock mean that it is time to get up or eat or go to bed? Does February mean that one should wear mittens or shorts?

Passage of time is also confusing. Sometimes persons with Alzheimer's Disease want to leave moments after arrival in a new place, believing that they have been there for a long time. Conversely, they can be involved in a repetitive activity interminably and appear to be unaware of time passing.

Finally, it is very common for Alzheimer's patients to be lost in the distant past. They may ask to go home, meaning the house where they grew up. They may search in vain for a "little brother" who is now 70 years old. They sometimes confuse a grown daughter for the wife. They may carry on conversations with loved ones who have been dead for fifty years.

Motor Impairment

Apraxia, the impairment of ability in performing purposeful motor tasks, may begin as simply as producing difficulty in dancing, biking, or performing other tasks in which the individual was formerly proficient. Later in the disease, victims will be unable to dress or feed themselves. Finally, bedridden patients are unable to perform even the simplest purposeful movement, such as scratching their nose.

Personality Changes

While changes in personality are not uncommon in Alzheimer's
Disease, these changes vary greatly among individuals. Some become
socially withdrawn, perhaps to escape embarrassment, to hide
shortcomings, or avoid anxiety-raising situations. Others become
verbally abusive, striking out at strangers and loved ones alike. It is not
uncommon for Alzheimer's patients to become fearful and suspicious,
accusing those nearby of theft, physical mistreatment, and other forms
of misconduct. In extreme cases, the personality changes could include
physical abuse by the individual with Alzheimer's Disease.

Often, persons with Alzheimer's disease exhibit an emotional
response that is known as a catastrophic reaction. Sudden changes in
the environment, strange situations and confusion can trigger an
overreaction in the Alzheimer's patient, resulting in agitation, anger,
and stubborn refusal to cooperate. The individual becomes excessively
upset, distressed, and difficult to calm down. At times there is no
apparent precipitating cause for the sudden shift in mood.

Behavior Problems

In addition to the aforementioned traits, there are numerous problems
of behavior that are characteristic of the disease. Behaviors often
mentioned by caregivers as being particularly difficult to cope with
include the following:

1. Apathy and listlessness brought on by depression
2. Clinging, suffocating behavior
3. Hallucinations and delusions (paranoid behavior)
4. Losing, hiding, and storing things
5. Restlessness
6. Rummaging
7. Sleep disturbances
8. Sundowning (behavior worsens when darkness approaches)
9. Taking things
10. Wandering

Progressive Nature of the Disease

A definitive feature of the disease is its progressive nature (Lampe,
1987). Virtually every symptom, every problem will worsen. This
progressive decline in abilities may fluctuate, to some extent, with

abilities remaining stable for short durations. However, over time, there is a slow, steady decline which ends inevitably in death.

Death is usually preceded by cessation of verbal and ambulatory abilities, stiffening of muscles (rigidity), and impaired swallowing ability. Incontinent of bowel and bladder, confined in a fetal position, oblivious to all surroundings, many Alzheimer's patients silently await the merciful arrival of pneumonia, the most common immediate cause of death (Lampe, 1987).

Stages of Alzheimer's Disease

The progressive nature of the disorder allows theorists to divide the course of the disease into distinct stages. Numerous stage theories exist (Butler, 1990; Gwyther, 1985; Powell & Courtice, 1986); these models may divide the disease into different numbers of stages and may include different symptoms in each of the stages. The authors are quick to point out that there is great individual variability and that the stages are less distinct and orderly than the descriptions would suggest.

Reisberg (1986) delineates seven separate stages in his FAST system (Functional Assessment Staging Tool), and further subdivides these in one of the most often cited stage theories:

Stage 1—Normal
No impairment observed

Stage 2—Forgetfulness
Very mild cognitive impairment
Complaints of forgetfulness

Stage 3—Early Confusional
Borderline (Earliest clinical deficits)
Inability to perform complex occupational and social tasks as easily as once did
(Lasts approximately 7 years)

Stage 4—Late Confusional
Decreased ability to manage finances, cook complex meals, shop and perform other routine tasks as well as once did; however, can still function independently
(Lasts approximately 2 years)

Stage 5—Early Dementia
Inability to select appropriate clothing

Difficulties in concentration
Difficulties with recent memory
Difficulties with past memory
Speech difficulty
Motor difficulty
(Lasts approximately 1 1/2 years)

Stage 6—Middle Dementia
Deficits in dress, bathing mechanics (such as adjusting hot and
cold water—bathing phobia)
Problems with toilet mechanics
Urinary and fecal incontinence
(Lasts approximately 3 years)

Stage 7—Late Dementia
Speech limited to a few words or phrases, deteriorating to one
repeated word, and finally grunts, shrieks or silence
Inability to walk, sit up, smile, hold head up
Loss of muscle control
Stupor, coma, death
(Lasts approximately 15 months)

Subdivisions have been excluded for ease in understanding. Still,
one can see that stage theories such as this, while imprecise, aid the
physician in diagnosis and aid the family in preparing for future issues
that will confront them.

Physiological Aspects

A great deal of research is presently being conducted to explore the
various physical changes that occur in the brain of an Alzheimer's
victim. The assumption is that an exhaustive description of the
neuropathology will ultimately lead researchers to the cause and cure
of the disease. However, since two of these pathological changes
(neurofibrillary tangles and senile plaque) have been known since
1907, one should not be left with the notion that cure will follow on the
heels of discovery. The following are the major changes known at
present.

Neurofibrillary Tangles

Neurofibrillary tangles are neurofibers found within the cytoplasm of brain cells (Powell & Courtice, 1986; U.S. Department of Health and Human Services, 1984). Found most densely in the hippocampus, they are strong suspects in the minds of researchers as culprits in dementia. Scientists are presently trying to discover why the filaments form the unusual paired helix configuration and what the precise makeup of the neurofibrillary tangle is. Tangles are not found exclusively in the brains of Alzheimer's patients. Parkinson's Disease (viral origin), Down's syndrome (genetic origin), and dementia pugilistica (caused by trauma) can all show evidence of neurofibrillary tangles (U.S. Department of Health and Human Services, 1984). This variety in disorders associated with the tangles makes it difficult for researchers to be certain of the cause in Alzheimer's Disease.

Neuritic Plaque

Neuritic plaque or senile plaque is an accumulation of degenerated neural material (Powell & Courtice, 1986). The core of the plaque consists of a substance called amyloid, an abnormal protein typically not found in the brain (U.S. Department of Health and Human Services, 1984).

Like neurofibrillary tangles, senile plaque is not the exclusive property of Alzheimer's victims. Plaque is seen in aged individuals with Down's syndrome, as well as normal aged subjects (Koo & Price, 1993). While diagnosis of Alzheimer's Disease is made on the basis of evidence of both neurofibrillary tangles and senile plaque, it is the high amount of plaque rather than its mere presence that identifies the disease.

Granulovacular Degeneration

While not a diagnostic hallmark of the disease, a third pathological change occurs in the brain of Alzheimer's patients. The vacuoles (small cavities) in the interior of brain cells (particularly in the hippocampus) become filled with fluid and granular material. As in the case of the two previously-mentioned changes, granulovacular degeneration is not specific to Alzheimer's Disease and can be found in the brains of normal aged individuals (Koo & Price, 1993).

Acetylcholine Deficit

Acetylcholine is a chemical that acts as a neurotransmitter that permits communication between nerve cells in the brain. There is a substantial decrease in the level of this chemical in the brains of Alzheimer's patients (Lampe, 1987).

Theories of Cause of Alzheimer's Disease

While a great deal has been learned about the nature of the disease over the past two decades, researchers are still unable to pinpoint the cause of Alzheimer's Disease. A large number of factors are under investigation in this country and around the world, but a handful of theories receive most of the attention. The following is a short description of these.

Slow-growing Virus

The disease may be caused by a virus that infects the brain and over time produces neurofibrillary tangles and other pathological changes. This theory is given credence by the knowledge that this is indeed the case with another form of dementia—Creutzfeldt-Jakob disease. While scientists have been successful with brain-to-brain transmission of Creutzfeldt-Jakob disease, they have as yet been unable to do this with Alzheimer's Disease.

Environmental Toxin

It is possible that some substance in the environment poisons the system. The most commonly suggested intoxicant is aluminum. Because the brains of Alzheimer's patients were found to contain elevated levels of aluminum (which has been implicated in dialysis dementia), it was thought that this might be a factor in Alzheimer's Disease. While current studies have been unable to demonstrate a causal relationship between the disease and aluminum, this and other environmental toxins continue to be investigated.

Immunologic Changes

Several abnormalities in the immune function of Alzheimer's patients have led researchers to study this system as a possible cause of the disease (Cummings & Benson, 1983). Once again, researchers are uncertain whether these abnormalities cause the disease or are a result of it.

Genetics

A growing body of evidence points to a genetic etiology for Alzheimer's Disease. Early studies demonstrated a family clustering of the disease, especially in families where the family member developed the disease at a relatively young age (early onset). *Familial*, however, is not the same as *genetic*. Family members can share both the same genetic heritage and a common exposure to the same infectious agents and environmental toxins (U.S. Department of Health and Human Services, 1984).

Because a large percentage of individuals over age 35 with Down's syndrome develop Alzheimer's Disease, Chromosome 21 (the source of Down's syndrome) has been explored as the possible offender. The apoE4 gene on Chromosome 19 is also undergoing rigorous investigation at this time (National Institutes of Health, 1995).

Multiple Sources

Of course, Alzheimer's Disease may, as in the case of cancer, be caused by many different factors. There may be different types of the disease (such as early and late onset), each with a different etiology. There may be a predisposition established by one factor (e.g., genetics), but the necessity of an accompanying factor (e.g., environmental toxin) to trigger the development of the disease. If this is the case, success in finding the cause or causes will probably take longer to achieve.

Diagnosis

At present, there is no single clinical test to diagnose Alzheimer's Disease. In fact, without biopsy (usually performed in autopsy) there is no way to be certain that Alzheimer's Disease is present. However, a thorough diagnostic examination is accurate 90%-95% of the time. This is accomplished by a procedure referred to as diagnosis by exclusion. Quite simply, the physician or team tests for other disorders known to cause dementia symptoms. Once these have been excluded, the physician is left with the diagnosis of probable Alzheimer's Disease. A thorough evaluation would include the following:

1. Complete health and social history

2. Thorough physical examination
3. Neuro-psychological examination
4. Mental status evaluation
5. Diagnostic tests (such as blood studies, urinalysis, electrocardiogram, and chest x-ray)

In addition, the following are often performed:

1. CT scan (Computerized Tomography)
2. EEG (electroencephalography)
3. Removal from medicine
4. Psychiatric testing
5. Spinal tap (used selectively)
6. PET scan (Positron-Emission Tomography)

Cure Versus Care

In the best of all worlds, diagnosis leads to treatment, which leads to cure. Alzheimer's Disease does not exist in the best of worlds. There is no cure. Tacrine hydrochloride (Cognex) and donepezil hydrochloride (Aricept) are the only medications currently available that provide even moderately effective treatment.

With uncertainty as to its etiology, it may be some time before a cure is found for Alzheimer's Disease. A massive research effort is under way, investigating potential causes and cures. Often, however, this focus on future breakthroughs serves to divert attention from the here and now. Researchers and physicians are trained to focus on cure. In the meantime, individuals with Alzheimer's Disease have need for care.

Needs of Individuals with the Disease

In the early stages of the disease, patients can continue to meet their own physical requirements, but nonetheless are in need of support from someone who will stand by them. They need someone who will answer their questions gently but honestly when they ask what is happening to them. They need someone who can provide some practical support so that they can remain independent as long as possible without endangering themselves or others. They need someone to provide emotional support when the nightmare seems overwhelming.

Alzheimer's patients need someone to help them plan—for their future and the future of their family. They have a need to be treated as normally as possible. Yes, they are slowly losing their *selves*, but this will not happen all at once. They need loved ones to continue to recognize those parts that they retain and to interact with them as fully as possible. They need help in organizing their daily life and finding aids that will help them function independently and be self-reliant for as long as they can. Individuals with Alzheimer's Disease need someone to provide love, intimacy and security. They need to know that they have someone whom they can count on in the future.

In middle and later stages, they have more practical needs. They need someone to help with household chores, personal care, health care, transportation and protection. All of this, and they continue to have psychological, social, recreational and spiritual needs in varying degrees over the course of the disease. And though they continue to need these things, much of the time they will be unable to express even the simplest of these.

FAMILY CAREGIVERS

Types of Care

Broadly speaking, there are two kinds of care that are necessary for the victims of dementia and their caregivers—formal care and informal care. Each of these two could be further broken down into long-term (for chronic needs) and short-term care (for crises and acute needs). Formal and informal care could be divided into instrumental (financial or physical assistance with concrete tasks, chores and activities) and expressive care (dealing more with emotional or spiritual support, companionship and other intangibles that express a caring attitude). While working toward the same end, these two broad types of care, or support systems, are fairly distinct entities that often operate independently, much to the detriment of the patient and caregiver.

Formal Care

Formal care is support that is provided by private or public service agencies at the local, state or national level. It is the community response to the family. These organizations may charge a fee or not, but they tend to have a formal structure and prescribed procedures for accessing and using their services. These might include services such as adult day care, chore services, home health services, and medical care.

Formal supports relieve some of the burden for the family. Sometimes they provide the kind of expertise in care that families do not possess. At other times, they perform some of the unwanted routine tasks of caregiving, or simply reduce the sheer volume of caregiving activity required of the family.

Services provided by these formal agencies, important as they are, cannot replace family care. By their nature, they must deal with large numbers of people in a cost-effective manner, which makes it difficult to provide the kind of individualized, personal care that a family who truly knows and understands this person can (Toseland & Rossiter, 1989; Mace & Rabins, 1991). The family shares a history with this person and a love that adds a unique dimension to the provision of care.

Informal Care

Informal care is that which is provided primarily by family, but may include help from friends, neighbors and church members, as well. Support from neighbors and friends tends to be less formal, often spontaneous. This kind of support is typically freely given or furnished in exchange for goods or services offered by the caregiver. Informal support may involve activities as simple as running errands, providing transportation or visiting with the patient or caregiver, or it might take the form of full care for the patient in order to provide rest for the primary caregiver.

Because each of these systems of care has obvious shortcomings, a combination of the two is desired. More than a combined venture, a coordinated effort is necessary for truly effective care of the individual with dementia. This would require someone to assist the family in locating and accessing formal services, as well as helping service agencies respond to the particular needs of patient and family. While this brokering service falls in the domain of a case manager, the reality of the situation is that the limited number of case managers available to families means that the task will often be handled as well as possible by the inexperienced caregiver.

Role of Caregiving

The word *care* has multiple connotations. Guberman, Maheu, and Maille (1992) discuss an interesting and important distinction between two such meanings: "caring about" someone and "caring for" that person. Confusion between the two leads some women blindly to the caregiving role. They tell themselves that since they should and do care about their family member, then it follows that they must care for that person.

In its broadest sense, to provide "care for" is to act in such a way as to assist or support another person with present or anticipated needs in order to improve a human condition (Wood, 1991). The most common example of this is in the rearing of young children. In the minds of many, care of the elderly involves, to some extent, a sense of parenting. However, it is clearly unlike that earlier role both in the nature of caregiving itself and in the relationship with the care receiver (Baldwin, 1990).

Many of the services provided by the two caregivers are similar, however, because they include meeting a full range of physical, psychological and social needs. Cicirelli (1981) provides a comprehensive list of needs of the elderly:

a) Homemaking (e.g., meals, shopping, cleaning)
b) Housing (providing living accommodations)
c) Maintenance (of house and yard)
d) Income (for food and other living expenses)
e) Personal care (e.g., bathing, grooming, dressing, moving about)
f) Home health care
g) Transportation
h) Social and recreational activities
i) Psychological support
j) Employment (helping to seek job)
k) Spiritual
l) Bureaucratic mediation (dealing with business and government agencies)
m) Reading
n) Career education
o) Enrichment (special interests and hobbies)
p) Protection

Providing care for the elderly can also involve ethical issues for the caregiver such as individual autonomy, death and dying, allocation of resources, and the obligation of family members to provide care (Pratt, Schmall, & Wright, 1987).

In some ways providing care for an individual is the same whether that person is young or old, has dementia or diabetes. One of these shared similarities is the potential for burden on the part of the caregiver (Andolsek, Clapp-Channing, Gehlbach, Moore, Proffitt, Sigmon, & Warshaw, 1988). Yet, within that shared experience there are differences, as evidenced by studies that look at cultural aspects of caregiving. Mui (1992) studied differences in emotional strain experienced by black and white daughters who provide care. Choi (1993) looked at caregiver burden in South Korea, and Kobayashi, Masaki, and Noguchi (1993) studied the developmental process of caring for elderly Japanese with dementia. The development of Alzheimer's support groups for African-American communities and Hispanic communities has been explored by Henderson, Gutierrez-Mayka, Garcia, and Boyd (1993).

Regardless of differences, one trend has emerged which is becoming quite common. The role of caregiving has been extended throughout the life course (Parks & Pilisuk, 1991). No longer the exclusive province of young mothers, not limited to the much heralded sandwich generation, caregiving extends well into later life. A study on the prevalence of caregiving in a large family practice clinic showed 10% of the caregivers, themselves, to be 70 years or older (Andolsek et al., 1988)

While there is general consensus on what is meant by the term "family caregiver", it is used in a variety of ways in different studies. In some cases its use is based on characteristics of the elderly recipient of care (such as one with a particular diagnosis or functional level). In other studies the number of tasks performed by an individual identifies that person as a caregiver or not. In most studies, designating oneself as the caregiver is enough to be so labeled (Malonebeach & Zarit, 1991).

It is this family caregiver who has finally gained the attention of researchers and, to a much smaller extent, policymakers. The nation has suddenly realized that it is family caregivers—not nursing homes and not hospitals—who are providing the bulk of care for the elderly.

Evidence of Family Support

Contrary to popular belief, only 5% of the elderly in this country live in nursing homes or other institutions. Conversely, that means that 95% live in the community. Approximately 5.1 million elderly persons living in the community need some help with personal care of home management to continue living independently (Toseland & Rossiter, 1989). Where does this aid come from? Surprisingly, this needed assistance comes from the family.

That answer comes as a surprise only because a myth has been perpetuated in this society which says that Americans abandon their old (Hooyman & Lustbader, 1986). Yet, research over the past 20 years has demonstrated that the elderly are not abandoned, neglected, isolated, or rejected by their adult children or other relatives (Marks, 1996; Merrill, 1993; Brody, Litvin, Albert, & Hoffman, 1994; Cicirelli, 1981).

Nearly all (94%) individuals over age 65 have living relatives (Hooyman Lustbader, 1986). Most live near at least one adult child with whom they have frequent contact and exchange of services (Cicirelli, 1981; Hooyman & Lustbader, 1986). They see those who live nearby several times a week and interact on a regular basis by phone and letter with those who live away. In fact, one half of all women aged 65 and older who are widowed, separated or divorced share a home with their adult children (Hooyman & Lustbader, 1986).

Rather than abandonment, there exists a pattern of mutual aid between parents and their adult children that continues until the physical and mental health of the parents deteriorate, and the balance shifts, with children providing greater amounts of aid to their elderly parents (Cicirelli, 1981). This filial support is one of the most widely reported phenomena in current literature on caregiving. The U.S. Senate Select Committee on Aging (supported by a host of researchers) state that the best estimate available is that 80% of the care provided for the elderly is furnished by family members residing in the same household (Mui, 1995; Miller & Furner, 1994; Dhooper, 1992; Andolsek et al., 1988; Parks & Pilisuk, 1991; Franks & Stephens, 1992). This figure not only applies to care for the elderly in general, but reflects the percentage of care provided by families of Alzheimer's victims as well (Kuhlman, Wilson, Hutchinson, & Wallhagen, 1991; Maletta & Hepburn, 1986).

While this percentage is impressive, the numbers are astounding. At any given time, 10 million adults in the U.S. are giving care to an elderly relative; 5 million of these are providing direct care on a regular basis (Baldwin, 1990). The majority of older adults rely solely on family caregivers for a wide variety of supportive services (Toseland & Rossiter, 1989). Family support has been reported as the most important determining factor in enabling individuals with dementia to continue to live in the community (Schmidt & Keyes, 1985). In fact, nearly 10% of the elderly in general, living in private homes, would be institutionalized if family support were to be withdrawn (Hooyman Lustbader, 1986).

Family caregivers do not provide this care without a great deal of personal sacrifice. Results of a national study showed that caregivers were more likely than non-caregivers to take unpaid leave, reduce work hours, rearrange work schedules, and cease employment to care for family members (Stone & Short, 1990).

With the wealth of evidence of family support for their elderly, it would seem that family members would be prepared for the seemingly inevitable role of caregiver. It is, however, a role that appears to take most by surprise. Sorensen and Zarit report that few of the mothers and daughters in their study had made preparation for care provision in the form of concrete plans and organization of services (1996).

Types of Family Caregivers

Authors typically refer to *the* family caregiver, as if caregivers are a homogeneous group. In addition to the great individual variability among caregivers, there are distinct kinds of caregiving roles that can be identified.

Most caregiving is provided by one principal caregiver, most commonly referred to as the primary caregiver. As the name implies, this is the key person responsible for the care of the older individual. Primary caregivers typically devote the most hours to care, provide the widest range of services, and take on the weight of responsibility for the delivery of care. They are in charge. If decisions need to be made, they will wrestle with them. If problems arise, they will be responsible for finding solutions. If quality care is lacking, they are accountable.

In the best circumstances, primary caregivers are not sole caregivers, but rather are supported by a secondary helper network. These can be other nuclear or extended family members, friends, or neighbors. Basically, secondary caregivers provide assistance and backing for the primary caregiver. This could take the form of taking over designated instrumental tasks, such as providing transportation, keeping the checkbook, maintaining the yard or performing certain household tasks. The role could, however, involve less concrete tasks, such as maintaining contact with the patient or primary caregiver or helping to locate assistance for unmet needs. One of the most important tasks of the secondary caregiver is to provide occasional respite for the primary caregiver.

While historically it has been assumed that existence of a network of secondary helpers would relieve the primary caregiver of much of the burden associated with the role, recent evidence appears to suggest otherwise. Penrod, Kane, Kane, and Finch found that the size, scope, and composition of such a network had little impact on the number of hours or type of care provided by the primary caregiver (1995).

A variation of the secondary caregiver is the long distance caregiver. As stated earlier, most older adults live near at least one adult child. However, because of the mobile nature of our society, there are a growing number of adult children who live some distance from their parents (Hooyman & Lustbader, 1986). This does not mean that these family members cannot provide many important services as long distance caregivers. Calls, letters and visits to the patient can make a big difference in the quality of life for the individual in the early and middle stages of Alzheimer's Disease. Emotional support for the patient and the caregiver is a critical contribution. Financial assistance not only relieves some of the fiscal burden for the Alzheimer's household, but makes possible the purchase of services to relieve some of the burden of care. Inviting the individual with Alzheimer's Disease for a visit, or making a visit to the primary caregiver's home can provide an opportunity for a reprieve from the constant ordeal of providing daily care.

Finally, caregivers who have reached the agonizing decision to place their family member in a nursing home need not give up their caregiving role. Rather, they can extend the caregiving role into the nursing home (Hooyman & Lustbader, 1986). They can continue to give support not only by helping in the selection, acceptance, and adjustment process, but by continuing direct care. They can provide the social and intellectual stimulation that is sometimes missing from the nursing home environment. They can provide personalized care in grooming, meals, or exercise, where nursing home staff may only have time for "institutional" care. Lovingly stroking the family member's hair while brushing, providing favorite meals or treats on an occasional basis, taking long walks with hands held are all ways of extending care into the nursing home.

Family Roles and Caregiving

Each member of a family has a role to play in that family. Roles are not the same as responsibilities or jobs that a person may have within the family unit. They may include one's responsibilities, but roles go beyond that, consisting of who the person is, how that individual is perceived, and what is expected of that person. It is the person's place in the family—head of household, mother, or the person to whom everyone turns (Mace and Rabins,1991). These roles evolve over time, and even after they have been established, they will change over the course of life. Dementia brings on some of these role changes in a family. Paramount in this reorganization is the acceptance of a new role—caregiver for a family member with dementia.

Typically the burden of that role falls to a single person (Caserta, Lund, Wright, & Redburn, 1987). Most often that person is a wife or daughter (Barber & Pasley, 1995; Kuhlman, Wilson, Hutchinson, & Wallhagen, 1991). While husbands (and less frequently, sons) do provide care, they generally do not assume the primary caregiver role, unless a daughter or daughter-in-law is unavailable. Men tend to take on tasks of non-direct care such as financial and legal matters (Mace, Whitehouse, & Smyth, 1993).

There are generational differences in caregiving roles, as well. While spouses may prefer to take on the role of caregiver, their advancing age and poor health may limit the energy, physical and financial resources that they bring to the role. Adult children, on the other hand, are often caught between competing demands of their nuclear family, their career, and the caregiver role (Pett, Caserta, Hutton, & Lund, 1988; Mace, Whitehouse, & Smyth, 1993). Therefore, when a spouse is available to provide care, adult children usually choose to assume the role of secondary caregiver (Hooyman & Lustbader, 1986).

Taking all of these factors into account, it is estimated (Greenberg, Boyd, and Hale, 1992; Stone, Cafferata, & Sangl, 1987) that caregiving responsibilities to functionally impaired elders are distributed in the following manner:

Daughters 29%
Wives 23%
Other females 20%
Husbands 13%
Sons 8%
Other males 7%

Other studies (e.g., Andolsek et al., 1988) produce different breakdowns, which can be attributed, in part, to sampling techniques and whether one is determining proportion of total care provided by each family member or the percentage of time various family members assume the role of primary caregiver.

The assumption of the caregiving role by an adult child is often referred to as role reversal. This unfortunate term can result in distress on the part of the parent and confusion on the part of the adult child. In healthy relationships it is not a role reversal that takes place, but a role shift (Springer & Brubaker, 1984). The child does not become a parent to the parent. Rather, adult children take on the filial role, which involves being depended upon to help meet parents' needs and seeing parents as individuals (mere mortals) with their own rights, needs, limitations, and life histories (Shanas & Streib, 1965). This filial maturity should be seen as a universal, normal stage of development, and its likely task of caregiving should be viewed as a probable role rather than as some anomaly in nature.

This sense of filial responsibility may be the result of parental reverence, belief in a debt of gratitude, or an expression of friendship and love (Selig, Tomlinson, & Hickey, 1991). Changes in society may have an impact on the strength of this feeling of responsibility in the future.

There are no rules, then, for who assumes the caregiving role, and under what conditions. Each family has to work this out for themselves. Sometimes this is consciously done; more often the roles simply evolve. Hooyman and Lustbader (1986) suggest that families look at the strengths of their individual members and try to match family members with tasks that emphasize those talents. They suggest that the following factors be considered:

a) Skills and preferences
b) Geographic proximity
c) Physical health
d) Motivation and emotional relationships

e) Other dependents

f) Time available (blocks of time vs. intermittence)

g) Tolerance for psychological burden

This kind of analysis of family potential would improve the quality of care and lessen the burden of the primary caregiver. Unfortunately, the distribution of caregiving tasks is not usually so logically determined. A number of more subtle factors come into play in selection of providers of care. One of these is gender.

Gender Differences in Caregiving Roles

The gender differences in the caregiving role clearly demonstrate the woman's more frequent, intensive, affective involvement in the care of her family members (Parks & Pilisuk, 1991). She is more likely than men to provide personal care and perform household tasks (Miller & Cafasso, 1992), provide help with activities of daily living (ADLs) and instrumental activities of daily living (IADLs) (Dwyer & Coward, 1991), and give up paid employment or reduce it (Mace, Whitehouse, & Smyth, 1993).

When spouses are excluded from analysis in the caregiving role, differences are still evident. The pool of caregiving daughters includes those who are married, separated or divorced, widowed, and never married (Brody, Litvin, Hoffman, & Kleban, 1995). Daughters are more likely than sons to provide care for their parents (Matthews, 1995; Coward & Dwyer, 1990; Horowitz, 1985). Within that role as caregiver, they are more likely to perform hygiene tasks such as bathing, feeding and toileting, care for parents who are more severely impaired in ADLs and IADLs, and express concerns for the emotional well-being of parents (Malonebeach & Zarit, 1991).

Being employed significantly reduces the son's hours given to caregiving, but has little effect on that of the daughter's caregiving commitment (Robison, Moen, & Dempster-McClain, 1995; Stoller, 1985). Sons tend to distance themselves emotionally (Malonebeach & Zarit, 1991). They typically take on the role of caregiving only in the absence of an available sister (Horowitz, 1985). When they do assume caregiving responsibilities, they rely heavily on spousal support (Malonebeach & Zarit, 1991; Horowitz, 1985). It is not surprising, then, that they report less burden in the caregiving role (Malonebeach & Zarit, 1991; Horowitz, 1985; Miller & Cafasso, 1992; Parks & Pilisuk, 1991).

This is not, however, the only reason for more frequent burden reports by women. Women are more likely to feel a constriction of social and personal activities (Miller & Montgomery, 1990). In part, this heavy burden comes from their internalization of society's assignment of the caregiving role to them (Parks & Pilisuk, 1991). "Socialized from childhood on to attend to others' needs, women often have difficulty refusing requests for attention and nurturance from employers, workmates, and subordinates, as well as from relatives" (Hooyman & Lustbader, 1986, p. 18). They become everyone's caregiver. And in their role as primary caregiver to their aging spouse or parent, they have a difficult time setting limits on their efforts and often refuse offers of help from others (Hooyman & Lustbader, 1986; Corcoran, 1992). They continue to give this fully, despite the potential for overload (Pett, Caserta, Hutton, & Lund, 1988).

Men and women approach the caregiving tasks very differently. In a study of caregiving husbands and wives conducted by Corcoran (1992) men were found to use a task-oriented approach, carrying out duties in a linear fashion, typical of the approach used in the workplace. Their focus was on the completion of the caregiving task in the most efficient manner, which often involved the delegation of responsibilities for everyday tasks to others and the purchase of instrumental services.

Women in the study tended to use a parent-infant model, taking on total responsibility for full care as well as nurturance. They tended to perform all instrumental tasks themselves, devoting more time to the task of caregiving. In effect, they enfolded the caregiving task, nesting it within other activities in order to accomplish more than one task at a time. It became less a task than a way of life.

Corcoran describes the trap into which many of these women fall:

The comparison trap is women's absorption of misguided societal expectations about the high level of self- sacrifice required by the caregiving role. Stressful, burdensome duties are performed as a labor of love, and personal needs must be sacrificed to provide care. Feelings of anger, resentment, and pain are wrong and cannot be acknowledged without intense guilt. The comparison trap works by reducing a social problem (caregiving crisis) to personal attributions of competence. The implication is that a person who is hard-working and competent can overcome lack of support and feeling of burden. . . . (p. 1007)

Thus, the actual burden due to heavier demands and the perceived burden resulting from women's perspective create a stress load that far exceeds that of male caregivers.

Yet, level of burden is not the only difference in stress related to gender; coping styles are unalike as well. Results of a study of 58 families experiencing the stress of caring for individuals with Alzheimer's Disease show that respite and social support were most important to caregiving daughters (social support for wives), but neither of these were important to the men (Quayhagen & Quayhagen, 1988). (In fact, respite had a negative effect on their ability to cope).

Burdens of Family Caregivers

Stresses

What are these burdens that caregivers experience and what are their consequences? Dependency and disruptive behaviors are primary stress producers for caregivers of dementia patients (Quayhagen & Quayhagen, 1988), but the burden is really much more global than that. It enters into every area of the caregiver's life: physical (heavy lifting; chores for two homes), financial (lost income from reduced employment; extra food, transportation and medical costs), social (isolation), and emotional (worry; guilt; pressure; not knowing exactly what to do) (Hooyman & Lustbader, 1986).

These stress areas serve as a basis for the definition of caregiver burden for George and Gwyther, who describe the phenomenon as " . . . physical, psychological or emotional, social and financial problems that can be experienced by family members caring for impaired older adults" (1986, p. 253). Considering the broad array of hardships encountered on a daily basis, it is little wonder that the term "hidden victims" has been coined to describe caregivers—the casualties behind those obviously afflicted with the disorder.

Source of Burden

Part of this burden, then, comes from the behaviors of individuals with dementia. These may be behavior problems, limitations in one's functional abilities, or cognitive deficits that affect the patient's ability to understand and communicate. These burdens may vary over the course of the disease. Instrumental self-care difficulties, for instance, begin early in Alzheimer's Disease, and basic self-care deficits increase with progression of the disease. Yet many of the distressing behavioral symptoms decrease in later stages.

The burden, however, can be attributed to other factors as well. The sandwich generation experiences some stress simply from facing the developmental tasks and challenges of mid-life (Yaffe, 1988). For many caregivers, it is not the actual problems experienced so much as it is the pressure that results because the demands of caregiving threaten to overwhelm the caregiver's coping resources (Toseland & Rossiter, 1989). Some authors (e.g., Vitaliano, Russo, Young, Teri, & Maiuro, 1991) have developed models in an attempt to explain the rather complex nature of the burden:

$$\text{Distress} \quad = \quad \frac{\text{Exposure to stress} + \text{Vulnerability}}{\text{Psychological \& Social Resources}}$$

Caregiver stresses are interrelated. The effects of one can impact another, which can compound the effect of still others. This is demonstrated in following example.

The financial burden of caregiving could cause a caregiving wife to secure a part-time job. This could lead to role overload which could cause her to become fatigued. Because she is fatigued, she may be more prone to become impatient with her husband, which could produce marital conflict (Springer & Brubaker, 1984).

The literature shows only a slight relationship between the deterioration of the patient and the caregiver's level of burden. A stronger relationship can be found with the quality of the relationship between the caregiver and the recipient of care, social support for the caregiver, and the way the caregiver copes with the cognitive and behavioral changes in the patient (Teunisse, Derix, & van Crevel, 1991; Williamson & Schulz, 1990). There is no clear link between the length of time the caregiver has served in that role and subjective appraisal of burden (Novak & Guest, 1989).

Consequences of Caregiver Burden

The caregiving role would be difficult under the best of circumstances. With little or no encouragement, praise or thanks from patient, family or professionals, it becomes overwhelming. This feeling of being overwhelmed impacts mental health in the form of depression, anxiety, guilt, self-blame, psychosomatic disorders, conflict in the family, marital discord, exacerbation of long standing interpersonal problems, and drug and alcohol abuse (Toseland & Rossiter, 1989; Mace, Whitehouse, & Smyth, 1993; Wright, 1991; Kuhlman, Wilson, Hutchinson, & Wallhagen, 1991).

A review of the literature by Toseland and Rossiter (1989) shows that many researchers believe that the caregiving burden also has a negative effect on health. Baumgarten (1989), however, points out that problems in methodology (such as small or non-representative samples, inappropriate study design, and absence of control groups) make it difficult to make any general statement about the effects of caregiving on health.

The strain of the burden of caregiving can, however, decrease the ability of the caregiver to cope (Kuhlman, Wilson, Hutchinson, & Wallhagen, 1991). It also increases the chances that the recipient of care will be placed in a nursing home (Lieberman & Kramer, 1991; Pruchno, Michaels, & Potashnik, 1990).

Abuse of Individuals with Dementia

This persistent strain can even push caregivers to their breaking point and beyond (Hooyman & Lustbader, 1986; Mace, Whitehead, & Smyth, 1993). In what has to be one of the greatest of ironies, the caregiver—that giver of heroic magnitude—can become the abuser.

Steinmetz (1988), in one of the first studies to focus exclusively on abuse in the family setting and gather data from caregivers instead of professionals, found that 23% of the 104 families studied used some form of physical abuse (hitting, slapping, restraining, threat of physical abuse, forcing food or medicine). Forty-four percent of these reported resorting to such tactics "sometimes", while twenty-two percent said they always use some form of physical abuse to control the patient when a problem arose. Abuse by caregivers was highly correlated to abusive techniques used by their parents in their family of origin. One of the most interesting aspects of the study was the frequent difficulty in distinguishing between the abuser and the victim. This was supported by a study of dementia patients and their caregivers, which found that caregivers who had been abused by patients were more likely to reciprocate with abuse of their own (Coyne, Reichman, & Berbig, 1993).

One of the most effective intervention strategies is to stop abuse before it occurs. This requires professionals, families, and friends to observe warning signs—to be able to determine when the level of burden is dangerous. A number of measures of burden have been developed for this and other purposes.

Burden Scales

Zarit, Reeves, and Bach-Peterson (1980) have developed the Burden Interview, Robinson (1983) produced the Caregiver Strain Index, and Vitaliano, Russo, Young, Becker and Maiuro (1991) constructed a Screen for Caregiver Burden that measures both objective and subjective burden. George and Gwyther (1986) avoid the existing scales, which are geared to a special population and therefore make it impossible to compare caregivers to the general population. Instead, they use measures of physical health, mental health, social participation, and financial resources to assess the burden of the caregiver.

Utilization of Resources

Most families have need for a variety of supports to help reduce the burden of caregiving (Baldwin, 1990; Hardy & Riffle, 1993). Mace, Whitehouse, and Smyth (1993) present a very detailed list of possible services for persons with dementia:

a) Physician services
b) Patient assessment services
c) Skilled nursing care
d) Physical therapy
e) Occupational therapy
f) Speech therapy
g) Personal care
h) Home health aide services (help with medications, personal care, etc.)
i) Homemaker services (cooking cleaning, laundry, etc)
j) Chore services (Household repairs, errands)
k) Supervision
l) Paid companion/sitter
m) Congregate meals
n) Home-delivered meals
o) Telephone reassurance
p) Personal emergency response

q) Transportation
r) Recreation services
s) Mental health services
t) Adult day care
u) Respite care
v) Dental care
w) Legal services
x) Case management
y) Information and referral services
z) Hospice services

While not all individuals with dementia and their caregivers need each of these services, the benefits of services such as respite to clients, family and community seem indisputable (Miller, Gulle, & McCue, 1986). Yet, utilization of community services has been surprisingly low. This has been attributed to the caregiver's perceived lack of services or lack of access to those services (Caserta, Lund, & Wright, & Redburn, 1987). "Both adult children and spouses are often dismayed by the lack of societal supports for their efforts" (Hooyman & Lustbader, 1986, p. 6). Caregivers often do not know how to locate services that they need; many times they do not even know that the services exist (Sisson & Gilbreath, 1987).

At times when caregivers need support the most, even informal support may be very low. This could be due, in part, to the caregiver's over-involvement with the patient, inability of family and friends to cope with dementia, or the loss of the caregiver's main source of support—the person with dementia (Kuhlman, Wilson, Hutchinson, & Wallhagen, 1991).

However, support does not appear to be important for all caregivers. In fact, it may have a negative effect on some (Kuhlman, Wilson, Hutchinson, & Wallhagen, 1991). Still, a much greater effort is needed to provide support for the many who desperately need and desire it.

Caregiver Education

One type of resource that is available to caregivers is education. This may take the form of formal classes or workshops, support groups, or printed or audiovisual materials. Format and quality may vary, but access to education and training is critical to caregivers throughout the course of the disease.

Heston and White (1983, p. xiii) make the case for education, stating that from their experience they have learned "that the more families understand about the illness facing them, the better they are able to safeguard themselves against its worst effects. . . . " Education needs go beyond information about the illness. For instance, caregivers who lack interpersonal skills (especially assertiveness) may find themselves at risk. The assumption is that training in social skills can increase assertiveness and social support and, thus, lower caregiver burden (Robinson, 1988).

However, lack of training for caregivers has been documented by Teusink and Mahler, Reifler and Wu, Rabins, and Blazer (cited in Maletta & Hepburn, 1986). Being the first professionals the family encounters upon receiving the diagnosis of dementia, physicians could and should take the lead in providing caregivers with the information that they need, but this is rarely the case.

Families often spend anxious weeks or months before some type of information and education is discovered. The content of this education and training varies greatly, in terms of topics covered.

In their manual, Powell and Courtice (1986) provide information on a description of Alzheimer's Disease, caregiver feelings (e.g., anger, depression, guilt), physical challenges of caregiving, psychological changes in patients, safety issues, nursing home placement, death and grief, and taking care of the caregiver. A guide by Heston and White (1983) has many of the same topics, but adds diagnosis, theories of causes, and treatment. Greene and Monahan (1989) include physical training (for moving, lifting and bathing), administration of medicine, and effective use of community resources.

The handbook by Sawyer, Ballard, and Autrey (1990) takes a different approach. It lists 16 management problems often encountered by caregivers, explains their causes and gives suggestions for handling them. Robinson (1988) lists social skills, such as dealing with caregiver feelings, asking for help and saying 'no' before being overwhelmed.

In addition to many of the topics previously listed, Gellatly (1987) believes that caregivers need a psychological understanding of the patient and an awareness of the interactive relationship between the caregiver and the patient. Zarit, Orr, and Zarit (1985) stress the importance of teaching problem-solving and make the excellent point that caregivers need most to be provided with the information for which they ask.

Regardless of the specific topics included in educational programs or manuals, the real question is whether or not they are effective. A review of 29 evaluative studies on support groups, for instance, (Toseland & Rossiter, 1989) revealed that while caregivers reported that the groups were meaningful, useful, and important, there was no clear link between participation and important outcomes such as alleviation of stress, improved care, or increased use of resources.

It is clear that evaluation studies are needed to determine how well education programs meet the needs of caregivers. However, evaluation studies alone will not accomplish that task. To know whether programs meet caregiver needs, one first has to identify those needs. None of the literature on education surveyed for this book mentions conducting studies to determine caregiver education needs. Most manuals or programs, it would appear, are based on clinical observations by practitioners. While this was probably adequate in the initial attempts at working with families, the time has come for a more rigorous methodology.

Positive Aspects of Caregiving

Even with the aid of education and other resources, the burden of caregiving is real. The almost overwhelming demands can take a heavy physical and emotional toll on the individual or individuals providing care. However, many people find that there are positive aspects to the experience, as well.

Baldwin (1990) suggests that it can be a time to reaffirm close parent-child ties or marital relationships. It can provide a feeling of being needed and furnish an opportunity to repay one's parents for the earlier sacrifices that they made.

Motenko (1989) asked caregiving wives about moments of warmth, comfort and pleasure in caring, as well as satisfying changes that may have occurred. Feelings of gratification with the caregiving role were associated with caregiver well-being.

Hooyman and Lustbader (1986) proclaim many potential rewards inherent in the role of caregiving. The opportunity exists for adult children to actually improve their relationships with their parents. This is a new role for each, and with it, a new beginning.

The touching that is intrinsic to the caregiving role can provide an opportunity for expressing love in a way that is foreign to some families. The experience of providing care can also be a time for discovery of strengths in siblings. It might just as well disclose strengths in the caregivers, themselves, and enable parents to recognize them as full adults, able to make real contributions.

The experience of caring for one's parents can provide one-on-one time, possibly for the first time in the relationship. Parents can express warm feelings of gratitude for the sacrifices that their children are making. Adult children sometimes come to accept their parents as real persons and forgive them for real or imagined shortcomings (Eckert & Schulman, 1996). The reality of the illness, itself, can have a focusing effect. A sense of urgency is experienced, almost demanding that family members deal with unresolved interpersonal issues from the past.

Factors Influencing the Selection of Caregivers

Individuals deciding whether or not to accept the role of family caregiver might carefully weigh these positive aspects of caregiving against the burdens listed earlier. But is one's acceptance of the role always the result of a conscious decision? If so, do other factors beyond the pros and cons enter into the decision? Are motivating factors the same for women and men, spouses and adult children? These and other questions concerning the manner in which caregivers find themselves in their role have only recently caught the attention of researchers. Some have theorized motivations, based on observation. Others have asked the question of motivation in a somewhat superficial manner, often as an incidental aside to the main focus of a study. Finally, a few have focused directly on the question, attempting to get at reasons below the surface.

Shanas and Streib (1965) describe in detail a sense of filial responsibility that healthy adult children feel as the balance of interdependence shifts and older parents find themselves in need of more and more support. Selig, Tomlinson, and Hickey (1991) take the notion one step further by proposing that this duty of one's offspring is induced by parental reverence, a debt of gratitude, or an expression of friendship and love.

Cicirelli (1981) suggests that feelings of attachment and feelings of obligation play a role in becoming a caregiver, but Edwards (1993) believes that regardless of one's personal motivation, societal expectation bears heavily on the decision.

Cantor and Hirshorn (1989) present a wide array of factors that may account for the why of caregiving. They begin with the values, attitudes and idiosyncratic history of the particular family and combine it with the psyche of the individual. Next they add societal and personal factors (e.g., availability of community resources and family members, age, sex, health, work status and geographic location of the potential caregiver). Also considered are motivating factors such as psychological attachment between patient and caregiver, family solidarity, attitudes regarding filial and familial responsibility, society's moral and religious values on family responsibility, reciprocity, inheritance, and continuity of generations (i.e., demonstrating what is expected from one's own children, in turn).

Researchers have confirmed some of these motivations, as well as adding additional possibilities. A study by Lawton, Kleban, Moss, Rovine, and Glicksman (1989) supports four of these (family traditions, religious principles, model for children and repayment). Other results point to degree of affection between caregiver and patient (Brody & Schoonover, 1986; Finley, Roberts, & Banahan, 1988), feeling of obligation (Ingersoll-Dayton, Starrels, & Dowler, 1996; Pratt, Schmall, & Wright, 1987; Brody & Schoonover, 1986), reciprocity (Pratt, Schmall, & Wright, 1987), and traditional views of assignment of roles by gender (Horowitz, 1985; Stoller, 1985; Matthews & Rossner, 1988).

A number of variables are reported to come into play in the decision of whether or not to act on these primary motivational forces. Finley, Roberts, and Banahan (1988) found role conflict, distance, number of siblings, education, income, and race to be variables influencing the decision. Stoller (1985) adds marital status, employment, and level of impairment. Birth order, family relationships (including those between siblings), and extra-familial ties requiring time commitment were found to be important variables by Matthews and Rossner (1988). These variables are influenced, in part, by the duration and intensity of the care that is provided (Himes, Jordan, & Farkas, 1996).

These and studies like them look, in part, at the reasons family members choose or do not choose to become caregivers. Few delve deeply enough to explore the process by which the decision is made. Guberman, Maheu, and Maille (1992) lead the way with a study of family caregivers in Quebec. After a thorough search of the literature, they were left with the conclusion that " . . . there is little empirical research that focuses directly on the question of why women become caregivers" (p. 608).

They did, however, use Lewis and Meredith's framework of three categories of caregiving women: those who consciously chose to care, those who drifted into it and those for whom it was a natural, almost inevitable course of action (Guberman, Maheu, and Maille, 1992). Through open-ended thematic interviews, they inquired about the circumstances and the contextual elements that were present throughout the process of deciding to take on the role of caregiver. They also asked what reasons or factors were involved in their decision.

The researchers chose to go beyond the rather superficial responses indicating that the family was the ideal place to provide care for relatives because of the bonds of love and duty one expects to find there. A study by Wood (1991) typifies the results one gets from casual questioning on motivation. The caregivers "believed that caregiving was their responsibility by virtue of the relationship or because no one else was available to assume the role" (p. 197). Eight of ten respondents said that they were the only person in the family who could provide care.

The efforts of the Quebec team were well-rewarded. Their results included 14 separate factors. The first six in the following list played a determining role, while the remaining eight were of secondary importance:

a) Love; maternal feelings; feelings of family ties
b) Inadequacy of institutions or community resources
c) Profound need to help others
d) Feelings of duty and obligation
e) Imposition of the decision by the dependent person
f) Women's socioeconomic dependence (has to live with patient for financial reasons)
g) Unavailability of other family members
h) Mistrust of nursing homes
i) The caregiving arrangement (getting help from other family members or not having to live with patient)
j) Religious feelings
k) Personal characteristics of caregiver (not working or not having children or "more resourceful")

l) Belief in the healing process (wanting to be part of any improvement by patient)

m) Dependent person's health (on waiting list for nursing home)

n) Family tradition (raised that way)

This study lays a foundation (both in the factors identified and in the method of investigation) on which other researchers can build.

SUMMARY

Dementia is a condition of deteriorated mental capabilities. Although there are many types and causes (known and unknown), the symptoms are similar. Memory impairment, along with possible problems in abstract thinking, judgment, language and personality, plague the victims and their caregivers.

While not limited to the elderly, it is more prevalent in later life, affecting as many as 15% of those aged 65 and older. The majority of the burden of care for these individuals falls primarily on the shoulders of family caregivers, who often struggle with the lack of coordinated efforts of support from government, friends and other family members. Many of these caregivers are, themselves, elderly. More than one in three women between the ages of 60 and 75 with a surviving parent provide care (Himes, 1994), and over a third of all caregivers are older than 65 years (Greensberg, Boyd, & Hale, 1992). Young or old, most are female.

Caregiving can be a positive experience in many ways. However, there is little doubt that it exacts a heavy physical, emotional, social and financial toll on almost all who assume the role. Just what leads to some individuals taking on that heavy role, while others find ways to avoid it, is subject to question. Beyond the obvious answers of love and family responsibility lie myriad factors that impact the decision. These factors are quite possibly different for different family members, depending to some extent on gender and family role. In order to help families and the professionals who work with them, it is important to learn more about the motivations and societal factors that lead to the selection of primary caregivers.

CHAPTER III

Methods

The focus of this chapter is the design and structure of this descriptive research study. The setting, sampling procedure, design, instruments, and analysis of data are discussed. In addition, a description of a midstream change in methodology will be presented, along with an explanation of why that modification became necessary.

SETTING

Multiple sites were used for the study. Two West Virginia cities, Charleston and Morgantown, and several small towns and surrounding rural areas were selected because they provide a population base large enough for adequate subject recruitment and have extensive formal support networks which have established ties with family caregivers of individuals with dementia. In addition, Parkersburg, Huntington, and Lewisburg were identified as potential sites in the event that more informants (subjects) were needed.

Informants were interviewed in the comfort of their homes when possible. However, an interview in the home would have created a hardship for some informants. When this situation arose, or when the patient's presence made it difficult to talk freely, neutral settings (e.g., library, Senior Center) were used. Care was taken to see that there was the assurance of privacy in the neutral locations. The six informants who used neutral settings appeared as relaxed and forthcoming as those who were interviewed in their homes. However, it should be noted that, with one exception, these out-of-home interviews were shorter in duration (as were the informal talks before and after interviews).

The in-home interviews were conducted in rather informal surroundings, with the kitchen table being the preferred platform for discussion. The same candor displayed in the stories of the caregivers was evident in the surroundings they chose to tell those stories. There seemed to be no attempt to "straighten" the house for a guest or to confine his visit to the most presentable room in the house. Pretense is a behavior unknown to these people or discarded by them. Whether this is an Appalachian trait or a perspective developed over years of caring for a hard-to-manage Alzheimer's patient, there seemed to be an attitude that said, "This is me, and this is my home. If you are to understand my role as caregiver, you must get to know me and get to know where and how I live." I was deeply moved by the generosity and the openness of these women who allowed me this opportunity.

SAMPLE

The sample consisted of 15 subjects, referred to as informants in most qualitative research, and hereafter simply called caregivers in this study. The sample was limited to adult women (over age 21) who are presently, or have formerly been, the primary caregiver for a parent with dementia. For the purposes of this study, primary caregivers are defined as those individuals who claim to have the main responsibility for providing the bulk of the direct care of the impaired older adult. Any question of that status by service professionals or family members would eliminate that person as a potential subject.

There was no attempt to limit participation exclusively to those caring for a parent with diagnosed dementia. Recipients of care were accepted as having dementia if their caregivers and/or service providers reported signs of memory problems and difficulties with judgment, language, personality, or abstract thinking severe enough to interfere with their daily lives.

The sampling procedure made use of a purposeful sample. Colleagues who work with me in the Alzheimer's network throughout the state were asked to identify caregivers who were articulate, reflective, and willing to share their stories. This procedure not only aided me in my attempt to reach the best informants, but gave me access to strangers by enabling me to build on the trust between my colleagues and those whom they nominated. No attempt at randomization or inclusion of quotas was made, as these would violate the principles of sampling for qualitative research (Morse, 1989). The sample was tested for appropriateness and adequacy throughout the study by the investigator.

While demographic information about the group of caregivers interviewed gives only the briefest picture of participants, it is a good starting place and provides a sketch which can later be fashioned into a more intimate portrait. Although the process used to select participants was not an attempt to create variety in the group to be studied, there was, indeed, a good deal of diversity among participants.

The average age of the caregiver at the time of the interview was 56 years, although there was a range in ages from 42 to 77 years. And while the average caregiver was just over 47 years at the start of care, one was as old as 69 years (77 at end of the role). Seven of the caregivers were married, six divorced, one widowed and one single during the time they provided care.

Most were in reported good health at the start. Two-thirds were employed outside the home when they began their role as caregiver. While just more than half lived in cities or towns of 25,000 or more, many lived in tiny towns or rural areas. There were only two African-Americans in the group; the remaining 13 were Caucasian.

On average, the caregivers had three siblings, although this number went as high as six. All but two of the caregivers had children of their own at the time they were caring for their parents. The dependent parent was her mother in the case of all but one of the caregivers. Eight of the parents were diagnosed with Alzheimer's Disease, with the remaining being undiagnosed or simply labeled as dementia patients. The caregivers took care of their parents for an average of 6.75 years, with one providing care for over 17 years. It has been eight years since some of them were primary caregivers, while seven were still providing care at the time of the study. They cared for parents as young as age fifty-eight and as old as age ninety-four. (See Appendix B for demographic data on individual caregivers).

While the demographic characteristics varied, the caregiving experience was remarkably similar for these fifteen women. The question remained: Did the same forces bring them to this role?

ORIGINAL DESIGN

The initial plan for this research was that it would be a two-stage study, the first phase being qualitative and the second using quantitative methods to study the same question and subjects from a different perspective. While qualitative research is a legitimate form of study in its own right, my original intention was to use it here as a means to identify variables for a quantitative study. Much to my surprise, I learned, as I moved through the research process, that what I first saw as a "means" soon became more intriguing than the "end" that I had hoped for. This led me—and my committee—to some serious soul-searching before deciding to revise the two-stage methodology originally agreed upon.

For purposes of understanding the reasons behind this shift in methodology, the original design is presented here. It should be noted, however, that the revised methods resulted in the elimination of the questionnaire referred to in the section on instruments, the conclusion of data collection before implementation of stage two, and an alteration in the analysis of those data that were collected.

Statement of the Problem

This study was designed to explore the following question: What factors influence the selection of adult daughters as primary caregivers of parents with dementia? It was anticipated that stage two of the study would produce a prioritized list of such explanatory factors, while stage one would create a starter list and add additional insight into the process involved in that complex decision.

Stage One

In the first stage of the study, the qualitative method of an in-depth, person-to-person, semi-structured interview was used. Using prior observations of the cultural milieu of family caregivers to develop initial, open-ended questions, I let early responses in the interview dictate the direction of later questioning. Interview techniques were employed that would explore the rich underlying circumstances and contextual elements of the process being studied.

The phenomenon investigated involves the factors that led to the informant's selection as principal candidate for the role of primary caregiver, as well as the mechanism employed to reach the decision to accept the role. Participants in the project were informed that they were taking part in a research study and that their full or partial participation was entirely voluntary. The purpose of the research was fully explained to each. All interviews were recorded on audio tapes with the permission of informants. Assurance of confidentiality of the identity of the informant was given to all participants and strictly guarded.

Stage Two (Later abandoned)

Months after the semi-structured interview with the individual informant was concluded, she was to be asked to complete a formal questionnaire rating and ranking factors potentially influencing her selection as a caregiver. While this questionnaire was to have a reading level and culturally-appropriate vocabulary that would ensure understanding by most respondents, I would be available to explain or elaborate upon any item that was not fully comprehended by the subject.

This questionnaire was to be administered in the same setting as the interview and, like the interview, would be conducted in the presence of the subject and investigator, alone. Participants would be asked to have the dementia patient (and any other family members present) remain in another room to ensure privacy of the informant and to protect the self-esteem of the impaired older adult.

INSTRUMENT (DISCARDED DUE TO REVISED METHODOLOGY)

The basis for the items in the questionnaire to be used in the study was to be the factors culled from the interviews of the caregivers in first stage of the study. These "reasons for becoming the caregiver" were to be grouped into distinct categories, being careful to preserve all of the unique responses contributed by each individual. This list, then, was to be the core of possible explanations that caregivers would consider. While the wording of the list would rely heavily on the original phrasing of caregiver responses in the semi-structured interviews, they would be modified and annotated to make them more "readable" and enhance understanding.

Participants were to respond to the items in two ways. First, subjects were to be presented with a Likert Index that contained the items mentioned above. Choice of response would range from strongly agree to agree, uncertain, disagree and strongly disagree. After completing that task, subjects would be asked to rank only the top three factors that they believe to be most influential in their selection as caregivers. In each of these tasks it would be made clear that respondents were to consider the factors' effects on *their* specific experience, not the selection of caregivers, in general.

ORIGINAL PLAN FOR ANALYSIS OF DATA

Primary and secondary thematic analysis was to be conducted on all interview data. The audiotape recordings of informant interviews were to be transcribed, and the significant statements would be extracted from each description that directly relates to the research question. After duplicate statements were eliminated, meanings would be interpreted and organized into clusters of topics. These categories would be referred back to the original descriptions in order to validate them. An exhaustive description of the phenomenon being studied would be produced by integrating the results of the analysis.

Originally, data collected from the Likert Index were to be subjected to correlational and analysis of variance statistical maneuvers. Findings and discussion would be presented in chapters four and five.

As it turned out, this statistical analysis, like the questionnaire, itself, had to be set aside. Data collected from stage one, which were originally viewed simply as pieces of information that would be useful in developing a survey instrument, had assumed an importance in their own right.

REVISED METHODOLOGY

Selection of Qualitative Methodology

While I may not have fully recognized it, the foundation of this study, from the beginning, was the qualitative research conducted in stage one. I had selected this method of investigation because of the type of information I was trying to gather. I wanted to understand caregivers "lived" experiences, as told from their perspective—their understanding of the larger world in which they lived and the tiny world of caregiving which soon set the boundaries of their daily lives. I wanted to hear the story in their own words. I wanted to learn what they thought was important to tell.

I did not want to undertake the task of investigation with the rigidly structured approach of a quantitative research design. That approach would surely allow me to gather data more quickly and easily, and it would enable me to better manage the information collected and manipulate the data with less difficulty. But to use that approach would mean introducing an instrument that presupposes a degree of knowledge about the phenomenon. I would have to enter the caregivers' world with a preconceived notion of what their reality was.

The simple fact is, I did not know. And the scant literature on the topic would suggest that no one knows. It would have been embarrassingly presumptuous to approach this investigation using anything other than a qualitative design.

I saw this research method as an opportunity for shared investigation—the subjects and the investigator working together to gain understanding. It would be a cooperative venture, a dialogue, an exchange. I would learn new things from them, but through my questions, my restating of their explanations, my summarizing of their stories, they would gain new insights, themselves. And through caregivers' feedback on my interpretations and their clarifications on my attempts at reflection and restatement, we would both learn things that neither of us would have discovered working alone. It would be synergistic, transcending not only our individual experiences, but our combined experiences as well.

I decided on the in-depth interview approach. Yet, I soon realized that my ten years as a support group leader, where I worked intimately with caregivers and their family members in their homes and in institutions, added greatly to my interpretations and my understanding of the information presented in these research interviews. During those ten years prior to the research, I participated in the lives of caregivers, working with them, caring about them, and sharing the experience with them. These ten years, then, served as a sort of "retroactive participant-observation"—a pre-research immersion—from which I could draw. It was nearly as helpful as if I had the benefit of being a participant-observer during the study.

Still, although I was comfortable in my role and confident in my method of investigation, I would not allow myself to rely totally on qualitative methods. In my heart I believed that qualitative research, by itself, was not scientific enough. I wanted hard data that would be respected by my peers. I was afraid that qualitative data, on its own, would be considered too soft, subjective, emotional. I needed the security of "objective" data. Stage two of my study was born.

Yet, this first stage was necessary, because this new research area was perhaps not ready, and I, as an individual, was surely not prepared for formal hypothesis testing. Rather, I would have to rely on my skill in synthesis and inductive inference to discover and describe some of the phenomena that might exist.

Rather than using a fully open-ended interview approach, I began with a semi-structured format that was topically oriented. This allowed me to focus discussion on the particular topics in which I was interested.

What I nearly failed to realize was that at the same time I was narrowly focused on discovering specific reasons for caregiving, I was becoming vaguely aware of a broader framework, an umbrella that brought together and covered a wide range of these seemingly unrelated factors. By keeping my nose to the ground, I almost missed seeing the umbrella overhead.

I was very comfortable with this qualitative approach. I knew my area of study intimately after working with it for ten years. I knew caregivers, and I knew how to talk with them. I could use their language, put them at ease, gain their trust. I was not an outsider. I had been in the trenches, and I had earned my stripes both at a personal level in caring for my mother and a professional level in working with Alzheimer's caregivers.

In addition, my earlier fifteen years as a counselor made me quite comfortable with the interview process and the use of skills necessary to help individuals reflect on their experiences and express their thoughts and feelings about them.

Finally, because of my work with families affected by Alzheimer's Disease, I had contacts to get access to subjects. Some I knew already and had known for years. It would thus be possible to establish the kind of relationship necessary for a productive interview.

Pilot Study

A caregiver outside the geographic area to be studied was selected for a pilot study. This allowed me to test the tape recorder and microphone, fine-tune the interview guide and demographic survey, as well as determine how I could best gain the trust of the Appalachian caregiver and retrieve the most information.

Data Collection

I implemented stage one according to my original design, and did, indeed, begin to gather participants' explanations for becoming caregivers. I realized very early, however, something that had only begun to become apparent in my pilot study. Implicit in that broad question that I was asking caregivers were a number of less obvious questions.

I was interested in learning about the factors that led to the selection of these adult daughters as caregivers for their parents with dementia. In less formal language this translates to, "Why are you the caregiver?" However, since informants often have difficulty explaining the "why" of their actions, I simply asked them to tell me the story of how they came to the role of caregiving.

Yet, some still had difficulty. There were too many questions tied up in that single query. "What is it you really want to know?" some asked. After a few short discussions, it became obvious to me that the original question contained a number of inherent questions, all slightly different.

"Why are you a caregiver?" is slightly different from "Why are you the caregiver?". Each of these is different from "Why are you the caregiver rather than someone else in your family?". I could ask, "In what ways did you choose the role, and in what ways was the role selected for you?". To what degree was the decision conscious, as opposed to evolving over time without a conscious decision being made? Was I asking what they thought their reason for caregiving was at the time they originally assumed the role, or later in the caregiving experience, or now that some are no longer caregivers?

These and other questions, posed to me by informants who needed clarification, helped me to frame questions for later interviews and forced me to think clearly enough to begin to conceptualize a number of constructs that would help me visualize the decision-making process of these caregivers.

Data Analysis

Unlike data analysis in quantitative research, analysis of my data began from the earliest point in the data collection process. During the taping of the interviews, I found myself inadvertently making notes of impressions formed as the stories unfolded. These notes went beyond the recording of non-verbal communications that would fail to be recorded on tape. And they were more than clarifications and annotations to explain responses of the caregivers.

I began, even during the early interviews, to see patterns emerge. Themes took shape. I did not welcome the intrusion of these uninvited images. I was attempting to compile a simple list of reasons for caregiving. These thoughts of underlying patterns seemed to be taking me off my chosen path. They were getting in the way of my original design. I recorded them more as a way of clearing them from my mind than intentionally analyzing the data as I was receiving it.

Having typed the taped interviews, I read them and made an initial attempt at identifying the different reasons given by the fifteen caregivers. I made no attempt at combining or refining these responses. I then returned to the transcripts to identify caregiver statements that documented the existence of each of the reasons on my list.

Duplicates were eliminated and nearly identical reasons were merged. Those that could still be documented became "factors", which then were assigned to categories composed of similar reasons. Samples from transcripts were then reviewed by a colleague to check validity and reliability of interpretations.

It was at that time that concerns about the original intent of the study began to emerge. Yes, a list could be produced. Yet, there existed a great deal more data that would be left unused if the analysis stopped there. The data were far richer than originally imagined. It was not just that the amount of data was greater; the quality of the data was more than expected.

It became apparent that the intuitive observations recorded and the underlying patterns that were emerging were, in many ways, more valuable than the reasons given by caregivers. A simple list of reasons culled from the interviews seemed to trivialize the stories of these women. The stated reasons paled in comparison to the promise of messages lying just below the surface.

Having sought the guidance and approval of my committee members, I decided to revise my original methodology—at least from the point of analysis of data.

New Plan of Action

Analysis of data did result in a list of factors—reasons as stated by caregivers. These factors and their documentation were produced by combining the vernacular of the Appalachian caregiver and the more formal language of the social scientist. They were grouped into categories through content analysis.

However, instead of submitting these factors to caregivers to prioritize by means of a questionnaire, as originally planned, stage two of the study was abandoned. Rather than conducting statistical analysis of data collected from a survey, qualitative analysis focused more intensely on identifying and developing the underlying patterns that had begun to arise. An attempt was made to determine if there were some theoretical framework that would link the stated reasons and the underlying patterns.

Three Stories in One

There are really three stories here. The first recounts my journey in discovering the richness of qualitative research. The second is the story of the caregiving role as told by fifteen Appalachian women. And the third is the hidden story of the complex issues, the hopelessly intertwined factors, and the created meanings underlying the picture of caregiving that is presented to the world at large.

CHAPTER IV

Results

My discovery of qualitative research as a valuable form of inquiry and a legitimate method of investigation in its own right evolved slowly over time. I was only vaguely aware that my perception was changing—that my understanding was increasing. I did not initiate this research endeavor with any expectation of that occurring.

I fully expected, however, to identify factors that influence the selection of adult daughters as primary caregivers for their older parents with dementia. I anticipated daughters in the study being able to furnish me with societal, personal and familial factors that led to their selection. I believed that they would be able to describe for me the mechanism or mechanisms at play in reaching that decision.

Eventually, they were able to provide me with that information—but not without a great deal of effort on their part and mine. Their journey to discovery was every bit as slow as mine. For most of these women, there was only a vague awareness of how they came to be caregivers. They were, in fact, surprised that I (or anyone else) was interested in learning about their caregiving experience and how they came to the role.

Those who were still caregivers seemed to feel set apart from the rest of society and were a bit dubious about the desire of others to learn about them or their ordeal. Those who were no longer in the role believed that their caregiving experiences were viewed as "old news" by their acquaintances, and that people were not interested in hearing a rehashing of the events and the feelings surrounding them.

Only one had discussed with anyone the issue of her selection as caregiver. Each expressed appreciation to me for asking the question.

Over the course of my time with these adult daughters, I came to appreciate them for a great deal more—their openness and honesty in discussing less-than-perfect family relationships and their own motives and thoughts, their efforts and hard work to search for answers and uncover areas of their lives that they might prefer to leave unexplored, their willingness to analyze painful relationships and relive the caregiver experience.

For some, this meant revisiting the raw emotions that accompanied their former caregiving role. Others seemed to have been successful at avoiding the emotional issues while dealing with the practical problems of caregiving that confronted them. Typically, however, the interviews brought a flood of pent-up tears. In reflection, the caregiving role was seen as bittersweet by most. It was described by many as being the most difficult and trauma-producing experience of their lives. Yet, most said that they had no regrets and would do it all again. Many described the positive aspects of the role as well as the negative.

The interviews were quite stressful for some. They needed help at the close of the formal interview to deal with some of the memories that they had dredged up and some of the issues that they had not resolved. I was grateful that my counseling background allowed me to deal with these unexpected circumstances.

Almost all expressed profuse gratitude for the opportunity to talk and to be heard, for the caring expressed, and for the insights that resulted from merely being asked the question—why you? Few had thought about it before. Some indicated that the question had just never occurred to them. Perhaps others consciously avoided it.

Many had great difficulty in even attempting to answer the question of why they had taken on the role of caregiving. The question seemed too inane to require an answer. They had become a caregiver because their parents had needed care. It was as simple as that. There was no question in their minds about what needed to be done. There was no decision to be made.

When I encouraged them to go further in their explanations, they continued to have difficulties. The reason seemed to them to be rather simple and obvious. It did not require further explanation. They were quite sure that everyone would answer it in the same way, and they were convinced that there was no sense in studying the question further.

With further prodding, they did discover other reasons to explain their undertaking of the role. Eventually caregivers in the study added significantly to these initial explanations for a combined total of 38 individual reasons which fell into 10 separate categories.

CATEGORIES

Several subjects may have used different terminology and phrasing to describe similar sentiments. While the exact wording may have differed, the meaning was the same, and, thus, they were integrated, becoming a "single reason" or factor. It was determined that each factor displayed enough difference from others to warrant a separate designation. The 38 reasons presented by caregivers in the study, then, reflect separate and distinct explanations. Certain of these 38 reasons, however, do share some commonalties. These natural groupings are labeled as the following 10 categories.

1. Logistical Factors—This category includes those responses that involve practical reasons that led to a particular person being selected as caregiver. These factors seemed to point to a logical and strategic conclusion in the minds of caregivers. They believed that the logistical factors almost made it inevitable that they would be selected as caregivers.

2. Socialization Factors—These reasons are based on values and moral teachings that caregivers learned in their youth. The individual's belief system was shaped, in part, by the family and society in general to include a sense of obligation.

3. Personality Factors—These are the personal characteristics of the individual that make them the kind of person likely to take on the role. While the traits may be as disparate as "nurturance" and "desire to be in control", they are all pieces of the caregivers' character, nature or temperament.

4. Parent-Child Relationship Factors—This category includes any reason that relates to the quality of the relationship and the closeness of the connection (present or past) between the daughter and either parent.

5. Factors Concerning the Healing of Psychic Wounds—The reasons given for taking on the role include attempts on the part of caregivers to resolve earlier issues in their lives. Typically, these unresolved issues related to difficult relationships between parent and daughter.

6. Exchange Factors—The reasons listed in this category suggest that present care is a way of repaying a parent for care they provided earlier in life or care they would now provide if the daughter were in need.

7. Factors Relating to the Quality of Care—These involve the more practical concerns related to the daughters' desire to place their parents in the environment where they would receive the best possible care.

8. Factors Relating to Sibling Relationships—These refer to the sometimes subtle beliefs that the daughters held concerning their place in the family and their rights as members. They build on the personal interactions and affinity between the caregivers and their brothers and sisters.

9. External Locus of Control Factors—The reasons listed in this category clearly suggest that the daughter saw her selection as caregiver as being beyond her control. The Fates, other people or other conditions determined that she would assume the role.

10. Factors That Benefit the Caregiver—These factors present opportunities for the caregivers to profit in some way when they take on the caregiving role. The benefits may be material, psychological or purely symbolic.

FACTORS

Typically, caregivers gave a single reason as *the* explanation for their selection as caregivers, although there were usually multiple reasons, often intertwined. As these additional reasons emerged later in the interview, they were frequently seen by the caregivers as being more important than the original response given. They often appeared to be new and somewhat surprising insights for the caregivers.

One of the difficulties the caregivers had in identifying reasons for their selection was the result of the ambiguity surrounding the caregiving decision. There was seldom a single point in time when the caregiving role was accepted. In fact, the daughters in the study rarely made a clear, conscious decision to become the caregiver. There was almost never a family meeting called to decide how the care would be provided. Rather, the situation just seemed to unfold gradually, and the daughter emerged as the caregiver.

For many, it was not, as is generally thought, a single decision, but a series of smaller decisions. Unless there was an unexpected crisis in the life of the parent that precipitated the need for immediate care, daughters found themselves helping in small ways to begin with. Over time, they provided aid with more tasks and then more assistance with each task. The daughter may have begun by simply handling the paying of bills for a parent who was no longer able to handle the task. Later, the daughter might discover that she could no longer be confident that her mother was properly taking her medication, so she offered her assistance with that task, as well. Preparing meals for her parent became the only way she could be sure of proper nutrition and have peace of mind regarding safety around the cook stove. Before long, she was "checking on her" in the morning and at night, just to see that everything was all right. She became a caregiver by default, and when full-time care was required for her parent, there was really no decision to be made. The commitment had already been made through a series of smaller decisions.

Daughters in the study were not able to verbalize this in response to my question of how they became caregivers. They gave more straight-forward answers. The above insight came to me as a result of my asking what I thought was an unrelated question—meant to be more of an ice-breaker than a probe. I asked them to describe the family situation before they became caregivers. It was meant only to provide some sort of context for them to describe how they came to be selected as caregiver. After the first few interviews, I realized that my perspective as investigator allowed me to see things that they were too close to see.

Other insights followed over the course of the interviews. I will reserve discussion of these for the chapter that follows. In this present section I will present reasons given by the caregivers, using their own statements, their own words.

Within the 10 categories listed in the previous segment, fall 38 individual factors, or reasons, given by daughters in the study, to explain how they came to the role of caregiver. For organizational purposes, those 38 individual factors will remain within their categories as they are listed in the table on the following page and described in the section that follows. The order in which they are presented does not reflect the frequency with which those reasons were given. For frequency refer to the final table in Appendix C.

FACTORS LISTED BY CATEGORY

Logistical Factors
   Proximity
   No one else available
   Helping parents remain in their own homes
Socialization Factors
   Duty to take care of others
   Responsibility to parents
   Responsibility of eldest child
   Obligation to care
   Woman's role
   Lesson for the next generation
Personality Factors
   Emotional strength
   Compassion
   Nurturance
   Take charge personality
   Patience
   Cannot say 'no'
Parent-Child Relationship Factors
   Closeness of relationship
   Love
   Relationship with non-demented parent
   Continuation of earlier role
Factors Healing Psychic Wounds
   Avoiding feelings of guilt
   Resolving poor relationship from the past
   Seeking parent's love
Exchange Factors
   Reciprocity
   Beyond reciprocity
Factors Relating to Quality of Care
   Avoiding placement in a nursing home
   Daughter's belief that she can provide best care
Factors Relating to Sibling Relationships
   Family just assumed that she would be the caregiver
   Easier to assume role than to fight with sibling

Avoiding guilt of asking sibling for help
Belief that none of her siblings would provide care
External Locus of Control Factors
Patient decided
Another family member decided
Role evolved slowly over time
Natural, normal part of the life cycle
Religious reasons
An accident, purely chance
Factors That Benefit the Caregiver
Financial incentive
Recognition

Logistical Factors

Quite often, logistical reasons were the first responses to the question of how these women ended up with the role of caregiver. It appeared to them, in retrospect, to be a practical matter. The reality of the situation was that when all of the circumstances were considered, it just made sense that the caregiving task should be handled in this way. The specific reasons may vary, but the thinking is the same, as the following examples demonstrate.

Proximity.

One of the most common reasons given was the deceptively simple explanation of proximity. It was often one of the first words out of their mouths. Living nearby made it relatively easy for these daughters to provide care, whereas distance was an obstacle that was difficult or impossible for their siblings to overcome. One of the caregiving daughters tried to explain it in this way:

"O.K. That didn't really happen until after my sister left", Arlene told me. "She left in '83. So, what I did is—they (Arlene's brother and sister) were both on the coast. I was the only one here. Our one other sister is—she passed away, uh, quite a few years ago. So I was the only one that was close enough to really do anything."

Arlene did not question her sister's decision to move away at a time when their mother needed care. "It was a real fast thing. She had been widowed for a long time. She went to California for a couple of weeks and came home and she said—I'm selling my house and I'm leaving. I'm getting married. So that was a real fast decision, right there."

Nor did Arlene consider the option of her mother moving to California to live with or near her brother and sister. "No. Because of Pap. He was still alive. He didn't pass away until 1984. And he was 91 when he died. And he had a lot of health problems, also. He had very, very bad arthritis. In fact, the last . . . I'd say maybe the last year of his life he was bed-ridden, because his bones were so brittle that you wouldn't even have got him up to take him to the potty right beside the bed. You could hear his bones cracking and creaking. So that was one of the reasons why we didn't even think of taking . . . we had them both in the dining room in hospital beds that last year."

Proximity, as an explanation, sometimes covers underlying factors. While the nature of these may remain hidden from view, their existence is evident. The given explanation is just too weak by itself.

Laura gave an explanation of proximity as her initial response. "Uh, I, being the person who lived next door, was the person that they would call when, uh, the stove needed turned up or down, a meal need to be fixed, or there was a mess to clean up, or something like that." Eventually, she became the primary caregiver for her mother. "I was within walking distance. The two other sisters were, uh, they would have had to drive to the house, although it was only a two minute drive."

Laura was, indeed, the closest child. Yet, it hardly seems that a difference of two minutes would be enough to account for her selection as caregiver.

No one else available.

The most frequently reported reason for the respondents ending up with the caregiving role was that there was simply no one else who could provide the care. On the surface this makes perfect sense. Obviously, if there was no other way to provide care, then the daughters in the study may have inherited the role for lack of available options. However, in each of the cases, there were alternatives.

It was not the complete lack of potential caregivers that led to her selection, but her belief that she was the only possibility. It was her acceptance of that proposition that left her with no choice but to assume the role.

   More than half the daughters interviewed explained that there were very real reasons why their brothers and sisters were unable to take on the caregiving role, thus leaving no one but them to take on the responsibility. In some cases, their siblings told them very explicitly that their circumstances did not allow them to help. The task would have to fall to their sister who was in a position to take on the role.

   With others, the message was delivered more subtly. The daughters reported that nothing was ever said by their siblings. It was just very apparent that circumstances did not allow their brothers and sisters to assume the role, whereas they, themselves, were in a position that made it possible to take on the additional responsibility of providing care for a parent with dementia.

   Sometimes the explanation was that the other brothers and sisters had important jobs that required long hours or the full attention of the sibling. At other times the women in the study explained that they were childless, while their brothers and sisters already had families to care for. Houses were too small or problems too big. Somehow, regardless of whether the evidence was strong enough to persuade an outside observer, these daughters were convinced that their lives and circumstances were in some way different from those of other family members. These differences enabled them to assume the caregiving role and prevented their siblings from doing likewise.

   There often seems to be a certain naiveté on the part of the daughter. It is as if she is an innocent who is incapable of seeing that which is clear to others.

   Callie was a wife and a mother. She and her husband owned and operated a furniture business. The circumstances of the family would not seem to lend themselves to caregiving any more than most families. Yet, Callie saw it quite differently, as evidenced by the following exchange.

Rick: *Robert's your brother?*

Callie: *Yes. And, um, Mother . . . I think she was having a lot of . . . starting trouble then. But anyway, um, Sarah and Robert got a divorce. That just left Robert there. . . . My sister and I were very close. But, uh, she had a lot of problems. Her husband was an alcoholic. And he held a really huge company job. It created lots of problems for Maxine. She didn't have time for Mother. For taking care of her three children and her husband. I don't think she had time to think about it a lot. Really. Uh. . . .*

Rick: So, Robert was divorced and had a job which took him out of the
           home. So, he didn't have time for it, and she didn't have time for it.
           So that left you with time for it.
Callie: Yes.

Georgia, who has cerebral palsy and gets around unsteadily on a
crutch, demonstrates the length to which daughters in the study carry
this perception. "My oldest sister came and she told me she knew she
couldn't handle it, and she wasn't going to leave her family to come up
here and take care of Mom. So I had to do it. You know. And my
middle sister, she . . . couldn't handle it. So it just left me and my
brother. My brother and his wife had to work in the District of
Columbia . . . so it just left me."

Bernice exemplifies the strength of this belief that there really was
no one but her to take on the task. She was convinced that if she had
not taken responsibility for her parents, they would have had no one to
care for them. Her therapist tried to help her see other alternatives, but
Bernice argued time and again that "It would not get done." Rational
arguments had little effect on her, as she explains: "And of course, the
therapist used to say—'but it will'. But I don't think it would." This
perception was reinforced by a belief that Bernice shared with Jackie.
They each believed that they were the only ones who really recognized
that there was a problem. They saw the changes in their mothers, while
others seemed to fail to see them or understand their significance.
Seeing the problems their mothers were experiencing, Bernice and
Jackie felt that they had to step in and provide care. However, since the
others believed there to be no problem, they felt no need to help out.

Jackie: . . . I'll tell you why. Because my brother and sister didn't want to
           believe it. See, they hadn't seen her. See, in their mind, they're
           calling, 'Well, hi, Mom. How you doing?' You know, and they're
           looking for some clues. O.K.? So they didn't have that. The whole
           sense of seeing her do baby things. You know, and then try to
           maintain a conversation when grown folks came around. You know. I
           mean, making stuff up as she went along. They didn't see it like I
           had seen it.

Jackie's description sounded very similar to Bernice's story, even
though Bernice's brother was close enough to observe the mother's
behavior.

Bernice: My brother that's here would never accept anything and really never went through all the stuff with my mother hating him and yelling at him and, you know, my mother would call me at work ten times a day and say how much she hated me. (Nervous laughter) You know, and slam the phone down and tell me how she was going to get me when I came down there. (Nervous laughter) You know, and he never saw. . . . You know, I used to go down to his house and cry, and he used to sit there and look at me like I was crazy, because she never did any of this stuff to him.

It may or may not be the case that others could not see that which was obvious to these women. However, it is not accurate to say that there was no one else to provide care. This statement diminishes the strength of character that the daughters displayed in taking on the role. There were other potential caregivers. They may have had reasons why they "couldn't" do it, why they were "not available", but they existed just the same. Daughters in the study consciously or unconsciously chose to accept the responsibility. Yet, few gave themselves credit for that choice.

Helping parents remain in their own homes.

Some of the caregivers did realize that there were other options, but they felt constrained by the consequences of choosing a less-than-perfect alternative. They believed that it was important to allow their parents as much independence as possible. They also believed that their mothers and fathers would fare better in familiar environments. Thus, they were reluctant to remove their parents from their homes.

Flora put it this way. "I did everything as long as I could. While she was by herself, I did everything that I could for her. To let her stay by herself as long as she could. Uh, I thought . . . and I did that because I didn't mind it. I didn't mind taking her. I loved to take her for drives and stuff. And I didn't want to bring her out of her own home, because I don't think that's the best thing to do. Out of their environment. I left her as long as I felt that she was no longer safe to be there (sic)."

Once the decision was made to allow the parents to remain in their homes, as independent as possible, then the factor of proximity once again became the overriding force. If they were to remain in their homes, then it seemed to make sense for the nearest adult child to provide the necessary assistance.

While this desire to maintain parents' independence is listed separately from the other two reasons that fall in this category (proximity and lack of other potential caregivers), it is apparent that there is considerable interplay among them. This pattern of intertwined reasons is seen throughout the interviews and in each of the categories. Few of the forces at work operate totally independently.

Socialization Factors

Duty to take care of others.

Some caregivers feel a general sense of responsibility for mankind. They are their "brother's keeper". This feeling extends beyond the immediate family. Some had, in their lifetime, provided care for in-laws, neighbors and friends, as well as their parents. They saw nothing unusual in this and believed that it was what should be expected of everyone.

Arlene wasted no words in describing what she thought was fairly evident. "I think probably, because that was the way we were brought up. Because, I think my sister even feels the same way. It's just the way we were. You feel that you ought to take care of people."

Only two of the daughters in the study expressed this general feeling of responsibility. Most of the women limited their sense of duty to provide care within the confines of their immediate families. Some made it clear that it was a monumental task and under no circumstances would they provide primary care for anyone except their children, spouse or parents.

Responsibility to parents.

Three-quarters of the respondents stated that this responsibility was inherent in the parent-child relationship. It is not something that has to be considered; it just is. It is not a responsibility that can be mitigated by extenuating circumstances in the adult child's life. Other things may need to be worked out, but this caregiving responsibility becomes the priority.

Dorothy stated that this was at the core of her philosophy of life. She had given more than a decade to caring for her mother, but she expressed no regrets. She had known that this sacrifice was a possibility that she might have to face. For Dorothy there was no decision to be made; this willingness to give is simply an intrinsic part of the parent-child relationship. "And I promised her in the early years when she had her heart attack, etc. I said, `Mom, as long as I can walk, I promise you I'll take care of you.'"

Helen echoed the sentiment. "Why, it never had been, uh, ever brought up not to take care of them. That's what, you know, we've always thought we'd take care of my mother and dad—you know, as long as we could. Me and my sister." Georgia stated her case as succinctly as she could. "Well, I felt like it's just what families does—take care of each other, myself."

Responsibility of eldest child.

There was at least one caregiver who supported the notion of the family's duty to provide care but believed that the responsibility was not evenly distributed among the family members. Isabel believes that the responsibility fell to her because she is the eldest child. Her parents expected as much and her siblings did not question it. Isabel, herself, felt that total care was too heavy a load to shoulder alone. She accepted the responsibility but harbors hard feelings for her brothers and sisters who stood by and let her carry the weight of the burden by herself.

Obligation to care.

Some of the caregivers described their motivation in a slightly different manner than those who said it was their responsibility. The difference is subtle. It has to do, in part, with the difference between feeling that one should provide care and feeling that one has to provide care. There was a sense of obligation on the part of these caregivers. They were just as loving caregivers as the others. They may have had many different reasons for doing it, and some of those reasons demonstrate that they willingly chose the role. But, at least, part of the reason that they accepted the role was because they felt they had to—they carried the additional weight of obligation around their necks.

They may have felt the need to repay some real or symbolic debt to the parent. They may have felt bound by some promise made at an earlier time, as reflected in this exchange between Kathleen and me.

Rick: *You could have decided something else.*
Kathleen: *No. She said long ago that she didn't want to go to a nursing home.*
Rick: *And you promised that she wouldn't?*

Kathleen: *And I said that she wouldn't. And as long as can take care of her,*
              she won't.

Woman's role.

While none of the daughter's stated directly that they were selected for
the role because they were female, several made statements that would
suggest that they were socialized to believe that caregiving was a
woman's responsibility. They would ignore brothers as potential
caregivers, implying that there was no one but themselves to provide
the care. When I would try to prompt them to consider the possibility
of males as caregivers, I would encounter a mental block similar to this
seen in an exchange between Bernice and me.

Rick: *Back before the time that she failed to recognize your older brother,*
              back when this first started . . . he was living in Maryland. Let's
              pretend for a moment that he wasn't. What if he were living back
              here?
Bernice: *My sister-in-law would have been there to help.*

She said that very confidently, as if she had no doubt, and as if she
wanted to reassure me that she would not have been left alone with the
task. But note that Bernice entirely overlooked her brother as a
potential source of help. She did not say that he would have helped or
even might have helped. She did not say that her brother and sister-in-
law together may have helped. She said that her sister-in-law would
have been there.

Lesson for the next generation.

Socialization forces certainly were at play in shaping the way these
women and their siblings perceive the world in general and the
caregiving role in particular. Some, however, were aware that
socialization was already at work on the next generation of caregivers.
They were aware that they are models for their sons and daughters. The
power of this modeling was not lost on them. Their willingness to
provide care for their parents makes a powerful statement to their own
children. The loving quality of the care that these daughters provide for
their parents is a lesson for the next generation in their families.

Opal alluded to this when she mused, "And you know, I think this might happen to me down the road. I certainly hope my children would take care of me when I get older. When I get old."

Laura is much more conscious of what she is doing, or, at least, more open about it. "So, um, I guess as this person in the middle, not only am I doing what I think I'm supposed to be doing in taking care of my parents, but I'm also doing what I think I'm supposed to be doing in teaching my children that this is the way this should be done."

Her strategy seems to be working for Laura. She is raising two sons who are already putting to good use what they have learned, and show every sign of carrying it forward to a time in the distant future when they might need once again to draw on the experience. Laura talked about her sons with great pride.

"My sons are—while they have been wild and crazy, and the older boy has made major gray hair on my head—he is a wonderful person, who is, uh, was wonderful with my dad. He could bathe my dad and do those things for me almost as well as I. And he didn't want to any more than I. But he was there and knew it needed to be done. Uh, when my dad died, he was eighteen. And, uh, he was well into his forties and fifties as far as life experience goes. We have joked in the family.

"This young man is now in school at West Virginia University. But he is in his third semester. He wants to be . . . he's taking art and architecture. Like mother, like son—which is a real ego trip. Both of them are just real talented little artists.

"Um, they also are very empathetic and sympathetic with the caregiving situation. They have been put into situations . . . uh, last summer, when my sister moved out of my mother's house—she had lived there for about a year and a half with her family—Jason, my ten-year-old would go up and sleep with my mother at night when she was in the house by herself.

"My twenty-year-old son lives up there now with his girlfriend, who is an older girl. And she does a good job—they both do a good job of taking care of things. You know, housekeeping kept up and things that Carie needs. Uh, we have our ups and downs and our disagreements, but for the most part, we can agree on what needs to be done. They're both cigarette smokers, so she can go up there and smoke cigarettes with them.

"It's a lesson that they need to learn. It's a wonderful lesson. I think that's what I was telling you before we turned this thing on. It is a wonderful lesson for them to be taught first-hand and to learn and experience first-hand. Not only the responsibility of taking care of these people, but the rewards of having taken care of these people. (Pause)

"The boys, they joke about the fact that when I get to this point, that they're not going to put up with me like this. That they're going to put cyanide in my coffee and just go ahead and get rid of the Kevorkian thing, so we don't have to go through this. And then, in the next breath, um, in a sympathetic tone, I would have my older boy look at me and say, 'You know, I really would quit a high-dollar job someplace else to come back here and take care of you. . . . '"

Personality Factors.

Some daughters believed that they became caregivers because they or their families recognized that they had certain personality traits that either made it likely that they would accept the role or made them good caregivers. Often these traits are described in general terms—'that's just the kind of person I am.' Helen's conviction that she had the personality of a caregiver was confirmed by a personality inventory she had taken years before she became a caregiver.

Helen: *I worry about older people. Not just my mother. Uh, anyone. And I do*
          try to look out for everyone. I can't the whole world, I know.
          Anyway, I just . . . I just take care of people. And I think . . . see, I
          done a test once at, I think, Vo Tech. And this is what it came out to
          be. I never even dreamed that I would take care of sick people.
          Especially the elderly, because what are they going to do? They're
          going to die. They're not going to grow up and get better.
Rick: *So this vocational interest inventory, this test, said what?*
Helen: *Said that I . . . this is what I should do—take care of the elderly.*

Many of the daughters in the study went beyond a general description of themselves as having the personality of a caregiver and identified specific characteristics that they possessed, such as those that follow.

Emotional strength.

A third of the daughters talked about the strength that was in them. This emotional strength not only helped them survive in the caregiving role, but was responsible, in part, for them being selected for the role.

In the following excerpt Bernice tells how she acquired her strength and how that character trait made her the most likely candidate for the caregiving role.

Bernice:	*He (her brother) just can't deal with it, I don't think. He couldn't deal with my father and I don't think he can deal with this.*
Rick:	*O.K. When you say he can't deal with it . . .*
Bernice:	*Doesn't want to deal with it.*
Rick:	*O.K. Doesn't want to deal with it. That's . . .*
Bernice:	*He might come see my mother maybe once a month, if that often.*
Rick:	*So, what's the difference between you and your brother in terms of personality characteristics or whatever that makes you able to be a caregiver and him not?*
Bernice:	*Probably because I'm a lot stronger than he is.*
Rick:	*Stronger in what way?*
Bernice:	*Uh, mentally and able to deal with stuff.*

Bernice proceeded to describe how she had been the one to make health care decisions for both her mother-in-law and father-in-law during terminal illnesses, before she came to take care of her mother.

Bernice: *So, I lost, you know, had to deal with . . . and we had to deal with deciding to take both of them off life-support. (Nervous laughter). . . . I've always taken care of everything, you know.*

This last statement is probably not much of an exaggeration. Bernice has probably handled most things that came along in life. She exudes a quiet strength that has likely served her well through the years, but which has also, in her mind, played a role in her selection as caregiver for her mother.

Callie recognizes a similar strength in herself. More to the point, she acknowledges shortcomings in her brother and sister in terms of this quality.

Callie: *That just left Robert there. And he didn't seem to handle it well. I think it's frightening to him. . . . It frightened her, too. . . . Maxine saw some things that she hadn't seen before. Like in the hospital. . . . She could not take it.*

Caregivers cannot always articulate what it is that separates them from their siblings in terms of strength. They just know that there is something different about them that empowers them, providing them with the necessary inner strength, while their bothers and sisters seem to lack the personal resources required for the task.

Georgia: *I don't know. I guess it's just because I had the get-up-and-go about me. And the personality. And I could handle it more better than they could because of the way I am with my personality and everything.*

Compassion.

Several of the women in the study believe themselves to be compassionate human beings. Again, this trait serves them well in the role, but is also identified as a reason for them being selected. Dorothy rather modestly describes herself in this way.

"I guess I'm a compassionate person. I cannot be mean to old people, children or animals. People in the middle line . . . I mean, they can fend for theirselves. But I cannot stand to see an old person mistreated."

Maureen not only identifies the trait in herself, but knows that others see it in her, as well. "Yeah. Well, I have a special compassion for these people. I really do. Here, I hadn't been working for the Aging Program very long. I was doing outreach. And we had a seminar. She [her supervisor] wanted to start a respite care program. . . . And from the start, she told the newspaper that she had a special—she could see that I was the one to take care of the people here. Without hiring someone else, she switched me over onto this."

Nurturance.

Some daughters seemed to be identified early in life for their nurturing or "mothering" qualities.

Rick: *Now, let me come back a second to that thing you said earlier about—the family's kind of always looked to you as the mother.*
Dorothy: *MmHmm.*
Rick: *I'm curious about the always here now. Was this always since you became an adult or was this back even when, you know, when you*

> *were still together somewhat as a family? Were you seen as kind of*
> *the person who would provide care even back then?*

Dorothy: *Definitely. Yeah, yeah. And always like, uh, well, for instance, if*
my brothers or sister had kids, I always took care of their kids. If
they had something to be done, they'd call me. Or if they needed to
borry a dollar, they came to me. You know, first. I guess because
maybe I had the biggest heart. I don't know. (Laughter) You know.

Take charge personality.

Three of the daughters expressed the belief that their drive played a
part in their selection as caregiver. They are the type of individuals
who don't let anything get in their way. They can be depended on to
take charge of a situation and see it through until the end.

"I'm the type of person that's . . . if something has to be done, I'm
going to try to do it to the best of my ability. You know? And if she
couldn't do something, I was always there. And I've always been that
way with all my brothers and sisters. Until this day, if there's a
problem, they always call me. You know?"

Patience.

Georgia's sister tried to care for her mother for a few days, but brought
her back almost immediately. When I asked Georgia why she, with her
physical disability, was able to handle her mother, and her able-bodied
sister was not, she replied, "I guess she just don't have the, the
personality and the, the patience and stuff like that, I would say. . . .
That's what I would say. That she just doesn't have the, you know . . .
because she would lose patience. They would lose patience and holler
at Mom for no reason at all when they would come up here. You
know?"

Cannot say `no'.

At first it appeared that the women in the study were describing a lack
of assertiveness when they said that they had trouble saying `no'. "I
asked my sister, `Would you stay with her two or three days?' `NO!'
So I guess there's some people can say `no'. You know the theory. But
I guess I'm the type of person that can't say `no'."

On closer examination, however, it became clear that it is the quality of mercy, not lack of assertiveness, that prevents them from refusing to help someone in need. Jackie set the record straight.

"And I told him. I said, `Let me tell you something. If somebody was to call me today, to tell me that you were dying and you wanted to talk to me, I'm going to move all Hell and high water to get there.' That's just the way I am. Now, why would I not do that for my nephew that just died or my mamma who needs me? What am I going to do? I don't know how to . . . that's it. I don't know how to turn my back on somebody I care about. I don't know how to do that."

Parent-Child Relationship Factors

Various aspects of existing relationships within the family accounted for some of the explanations of caregivers. The following reasons for caring are a result of positive relationships between family members.

Closeness of relationship.

Two-thirds of the daughters interviewed stated that the quality of the relationship between them and their dependent parents played an integral role in their desire to provide care for their mothers and fathers. They spoke of the special nature of the relationship. It seemed to them to go beyond the typical parent-child relationship. The daughters in this category believed that they had a special place in the hearts of their parents. Even in a family full of much-loved children, they and their parents shared a special bond that inextricably linked them together.

Isabel tried to explain the difference between her relationship and her siblings' relationship with their parents:

"Well, at Christmas times and Thanksgiving and Valentine's Day and every holiday time, I gave Mom and Dad a card or a flower or a gift. They didn't send them nothing. They didn't never call them on the phone. And they wouldn't come. They wouldn't call Mom and Dad on the phone. Mom would have to call them if she heard from them. And her telephone bill was always big because she was all the time calling them. She'd call them five and six times a day, not realizing that she had done it."

It was Isabel, however, on whom her parents could depend. She would never let them down. She knew it and they knew it.

In Maureen's family it wasn't a case of a poor relationship with some children and a good one with others. She, her two sisters and brother all had a loving relationship with their father. Still, hers was unique.

"I was kind of Daddy's favorite girl. Yeah. My dad and I sang together for years. He taught me how to sing. We sang Gospel songs. Gospel music. My dad was choir director for years. So, uh, and I always went with him. He used to teach singing schools. This was probably something you never heard of. He taught shape note music. . . . My dad and I had a special relationship because I had been close to him through music and through singing. My dad always took a special interest in me. The other two daughters didn't seem to be that interested in singing. And, uh, but he did, you know. And I feel like that . . . I was with him a lot. We went to church together an awful lot, and uh, and he always told me he . . . that he was proud of me."

This special relationship that daughters like Maureen shared with their parents carried with it a feeling that they were somehow unique within the family. It was a feeling of extra commitment, uncommon devotion. This devotion was not demanded, but given freely, and ultimately resulted in their willing acceptance of the role of caregiver.

Love.

Some of the daughters interviewed described this relationship in even stronger terms. They gave it a specific label and offered this reason as the basis for their decision to give themselves to the role of caregiving. They did it out of love.

For most, it seemed so obvious that they barely mentioned. Nellie went into great detail describing other reasons. But on this topic, she succinctly explained, "Well, I love her. She's my mother." Most of the other caregivers were equally parsimonious with their words on the subject. It seemed as though there was little need for elaboration.

Some, however, seemed almost unaware of this as part of their motivation. Laura appeared almost surprised by the realization that came over her as we talked late into the evening, and I asked her if there were any other reasons that she could share with me.

"Well, I don't know whether I touched on this or not. And I don't know whether I've ever actually verbalized this in prior discussions. And just sitting here, as you ask me this, it probably . . . I actually think I'm doing these things because I love these people (her parents). There are things again, there, that—I have to repeat—that I didn't like and don't like now. But that I do love them, and I feel that because I love— I mean, I love my children, and I do things for them, and I don't like them some days. And she loves me and she did things for me, even though she certainly didn't like some of the things that I did. And that's . . . you know, I guess I just love them. . . . And because I love her, I would want to do these things for her. . . .

"We laugh and joke sometimes about me doing it for spite or for payback or things. I mean, you know, you can joke about that, but I don't think that's really seriously why I'm doing it. I wouldn't be as calm and mellow and in charge of what's going on if I were doing this out of some negative motive. I believe that I do just love them.

"But I've not ever actually expressed that. I mean, I tell her sometimes that I love her. And she says that to me. So, I guess that's . . . uh, I guess that is a reason. Have you had other people tell you that reason?"

Relationship with non-demented parent.

Laura provides care for her mother, in part, because she loves her. But her reasons go beyond her relationship with her mother and are somehow connected to her feelings for her father who died a few years ago.

"I think that . . . um, I speak to my father frequently, now. There's a set of wind chimes on the front porch that are him speaking to me when it's right for him to speak to me. There's a set of wind chimes in my back yard that came from Gertrude, the old woman I mentioned earlier who died. And there are times when I'm really angry or frustrated or harried or something like that. And one of those chimes will ring my way, and I'll think, `Ah, O.K. These people are speaking to me. Calm down. I'm not in this by myself.' And I'm doing this because I love him. And because he loved her. He adored her. Yeah, he spoiled her beyond anything I can describe to you. And that he would want me to do these things. And because I love him, I would want to do these things for him."

Continuation of earlier role.

Three-fifths of the caregivers described their caregiving relationship with their parents as a role that was not entirely new to them. They had taken on this function at various times in the lives of their parents—

before dementia had set in. It was easy to slip back into this role when the need presented itself once more. They were familiar with it, if not entirely comfortable. Others in the family, including the patients, were content to allow these daughters to resume or continue the role.

Sometimes the earlier caregiving role was not with the parent who would later be diagnosed with dementia, as evidenced by this exchange between Bernice and me.

Rick: *When I asked you before, 'Why did this happen to fall to you?', did you say, 'The same thing happened to me when my dad got sick'?*

Bernice: *MmmHmm.*

Rick: *So you had this role earlier. This would have been . . .*

Bernice: *Twelve years ago. Yeah.*

Rick: *When your father had cancer, you became the person responsible . . .*

Bernice: *Yeah, because my brother didn't want to do it—who lived here. And then the other one was away. And I kept him in communications, but I was the one that had to sit with the doctors and decide what we were going to do for him. I'm the one that had to, you know, decide whether we were going to do the surgery. And, I mean, their point was, 'Whatever you think.' I'm the one that sat down and let the doctors draw me diagrams and, you know, tell what exactly his diagnosis was and what his chances were. And I'm the one that took him to his treatments. He didn't have radiation treatment, but he had those radiation implants put in the tumor. That, uh, I had to take him back for them just to examine him every so often. But I did all that. (Nervous laughter)*

Other caregivers assumed the caregiving role for their parents well before dementia had set in. Often the ailment was relatively minor, but the caregiving behavior was becoming well-established. Jackie described such a sequence of events.

Jackie: *My mother hurt her leg years ago. I mean, even in the midst of my anorexia. O.K. She hurt herself years ago. And so my thing was, "O.K., fine." I was in Detroit. "I'm going home and I'm going to take care of Mom for two weeks." You know, so I took off from my job. Because she had surgery on her knee. Well I did that. And I came home. . . .*

Rick: A few years ago you were experiencing anorexia and you were off
          somewhere. And your mother hurt her leg. And you came back. You
          said, "I've got to go take care of my mom." And you came back to
          take care of her during that time?

Jackie: MmmHmm. MmmHmm.

Rick: So you're really ... that was kind of like a rehearsal for this. You
          really went through this. I mean, it was a temporary thing but ...

Jackie: And that's ...

Rick: She needed help: 'I'm the one. I'm the one to take care of her.'

Jackie: Yeah, right. And you know, even then the deal was that all of us
          would take two weeks. And I came for my two weeks and then nobody
          else wanted to. My sister was living here then. O.K. So she was able
          to look in on her. But she wasn't going to take care of her.

Many times, the shift from helpful daughter to caregiver was so
gradual that it almost went unnoticed. Nellie moved from New Jersey
to stay temporarily with her mother out of general concern. A
daughter-in-law and her three children were living with Nellie's mother
at the time. Nellie was concerned about the way 'they talked to her and
treated her'. She decided to investigate.

Nellie: And at that time she was—as I say, she had a little trouble walking.
          She couldn't walk through the mall without resting often. Her mind
          was good, was good.

Rick: So you actually began to care for her before she developed ...

Nellie: Well, I actually wasn't caring for her. I was doing the cleaning and
          her wash. She could do it, but I just did it ... And finally, well, my
          sister-in-law ... my niece got pregnant. And she got upset with my
          mother because she thought that she was going to have her father,
          who she doesn't see, come up and eat dinner. So she's cursing at my
          mother, and finally my mother just told them, 'I think you have to
          find another place to live.' And so they moved. And that upset her
          terribly. I think that really got her. And she's seventy- eight, and for
          her granddaughter to get pregnant without being married—that, to
          her, is like the end of the world. So I think all this together, plus they
          weren't speaking to their father. And he wasn't allowed to come up
          to her house when they were home. This is his mother. So, you know,
          I think all that stress and just constantly everybody bickering. And
          him making sure their car's not there before he could pull in to come
          and see my mother. You know, it was ... and I think it got her

started with the strokes. I think she had had some strokes before, because, like I say, she was having some trouble with her equilibrium.

Rick: *She was doing all right with a little help from you . . .*

Nellie: *Mentally, mentally. Yeah.*

Rick: *. . . in terms of you preparing some meals, maybe, and doing the laundry and things like that—some household chores . . .*

Nellie: *Yeah. She could have done it, but, you know, she's seventy-five. I figured, 'I'm not working.' You know. And we went out. We'd have fun. You know, we'd go for a walk in the evening, sit on the porch and have a gay old time.. And I think it was about September. She started like falling, and she couldn't get herself up. So, uh, and even if you would get her partly up, she's as heavy as I am. So for me to do it is impossible. A neighbor or somebody would come, and like pick her up, and say, 'Now put your feet on the floor.' And, see, she couldn't seem to understand that in order to stand, she had to put her feet down. She'd just lay there. You know. I think she fell five or six times. And finally, in December, I said, 'This is it.' She fell in the yard, and I couldn't get her up for anything. I said, 'We're going to the emergency room right now.' So we went, and they kept her.*

Rick: *You then found that she had had a stroke.*

Nellie: *Had had numerous strokes. And the hardening of the arteries. And since then it's just been, you know, slowly, slowly getting worse. And with the hardening of the arteries that won't get better. It will only get worse.*

And as Nellie's mother worsened, the role of caregiver grew. Day by day, Nellie took on more and more responsibility for her mother's well-being. What began as a mutual relationship between mother and daughter turned into a role of dependency for the mother and a full-time job for Nellie.

Factors Healing Psychic Wounds

The burdens that can come with caregiving are so enormous that we can easily overlook difficulties that these daughters experienced in their lives before they took on the role of providing for their parents. While some of the daughters described near-idyllic childhoods and young adulthoods, others recalled their youths in less nostalgic terms. Their lives and relationships had been tumultuous at times, and they found themselves at mid-life working to resolve earlier issues at the very time they were presented with the question of care for their parents. For some, the role of caregiving became a vehicle for working through some thorny concerns.

Avoiding feelings of guilt.

A few of the daughters interviewed wondered whether it was guilt that really led them to their present position. "Am I doing this for her or out of my own guilt?", they asked. One expressed a strong dislike for her mother and suggested that placing herself in this new relationship with her might be a way of trying to learn how to forgive herself.

At the same time that she ranted and raved about all of the reasons for disliking her mother, her strong love for her shone through in the form of silent tears and looks of longing. It was too late for her mother and her together to resolve whatever stood between them. Her mother could no longer contribute to that process. The daughter was left to work this out on her own. She may or may not be successful, but she was not going to add to the internal turmoil by failing to perform her daughterly duties at this point in her life.

Resolving poor relationship from the past.

Laura has, at times, led what she believes others see as a wild and crazy existence. She is an artist, with the stereotypic "artist personality and lifestyle". She would have it no other way and, indeed, takes some pride in the fact. Still, she suggests that her behavior sometimes caused a strain in her relationship with her mother.

Laura: *I guess part of it is a sociological thing that . . . because I was a divorced mother, did not stay successfully married. I was an artist. I went to work for the power company right out of high school. Then, later on, when I had Jason, and I wasn't married when I had him. I mean, all of these things that I have done. . . .*

Laura is hoping that the care that she is now providing for her mother demonstrates that the grief that she may have caused her earlier was not intentional. She was just different from her mother. She still is. Yet her willingness to give to her mother when she needs it most helps Laura to resolve some things in her mind, even if it may be too late to establish the kind of relationship that she would like to have with her mother.

Jackie, a therapist herself, looked to the caregiving role as a means to understanding a destructive relationship that threatens her existence still today.

"I called my girlfriend and I say, `Janey, I have to separate my feelings—the anger and the madness—and separate that and know that I'm making the right decision, O.K.? Because I'm, still real angry at my mom.' You know. Because basically, she abused me and she abandoned me. Period. Period. You know. So now I'm wondering, am I abandoning her if I put her in a home? Though she's about to set the place afire. Right? Or am I abandoning her by taking her pills when she wants control? Or taking her car when she cannot drive? You understand what I'm saying? I don't know how to be. But I need to learn how to be. You understand what I'm saying. . . . to finish up my own therapy."

Jackie's relationship with her mother appears to have been poor since early in her life. They have done battle often, each hurting the other. The playing field was fairly level. Now, however, the field has shifted. There is no longer any contest; Jackie has an arsenal of weapons at her disposal, while her mother is almost completely defenseless. Thus, Jackie feels that she must constantly monitor her actions.

Is she acting out of love when she restricts her mother's activities, or is she repaying her mother for the unkind cuts that she received in her youth? And even if her motives are pure and she is providing quality care, Jackie feels that it is unfair to find that when she has finally reached the point in her life where she is an equal adult and can stand up to her mother, there is no one there to stand up to.

Seeking parent's love.

This therapy that Jackie needs to finish up centers on the issue of her dire need for her parents' love. She lost the opportunity for her father's love when her mother turned him out after numerous flagrant episodes of adultery.

"I can remember when my Mom . . . I was my daddy's pet, so to speak. And Mamma and Daddy got a divorce when I was like eight. And the way I remember it . . . and my daddy, I mean, my daddy, he had a lot of girlfriends. He used to take me to their house. Take me. So.

When my mamma put him out finally . . . we had this big old pot-bellied stove in the middle of the room. And My daddy was walking around this pot-bellied stove, and I was right in the corner, crying. And Mamma was laughing. And throwing his clothes at him, O.K.?

"So my idea of men was that it was O.K. to cheat, O.K.? It was all right. Because my daddy did it. And always pick weak men. Right? Two husbands. Both weak. One wouldn't work and one was a drug addict, who is now in jail because he committed murder twice. He killed two people, O.K.? My daddy was weak. See? I seen him weak with other women, but I seen him crying after my mom. And I was a little girl. And he was crying, 'Please don't leave me.' You see. And all of these things you play back in your head at this point. You know. So, here I am now. And Mamma was the strong one."

Jackie couldn't get the love she needed from her father, nor from the relationships she attempted to form with men in her adult life. But more than anything else, she wanted love from her mother—the strong one in the family. It was never to be.

"There was a . . . when I went to California, I was anorexic. And bulimic. I weighed 92 pounds. I mean, I was sick. I was sick. I had tried suicide. O.K.? And I know it was all because of the lack of whatever my mamma didn't give me."

Not only was Jackie unable to get the love she needed from her mother when she was growing up, but she was unsuccessful even as an adult in securing the most meager morsel of warmth.

"I was forty years old, and she had called me up with her old ragging, you know. She'd call me up. 'That's what kind of daughter you are. You've always never been no good. Never will be no good. You never been no good.' And I said, 'Mamma.' I was forty years old. I said, 'Mamma, I'm sitting here contemplating suicide. And I don't have time for you.' Boing! I didn't call her for a long time."

Jackie has spent her full life trying to win the approval of a woman who will never give it. Even as she gives her entire life to the role of caregiver at this point, she knows that it will not gain her what she wants most.

"Even now. Even now. I look at her. And, I mean, it would be nice if she'd just say, 'Oh, this is nice. Thank you for doing this good job.' And she's not going to do that. O.K.? She's just not going to do that."

Still, that does not stop Jackie from trying. She has given up a good job as a counselor, a full life in New York, and an opportunity to live near her children to move to West Virginia and provide 24-hour a day care to her mother. And she says, "I really want to do this. I really want Mamma to like me."

Exchange Factors

Some caregivers viewed their role as part of an exchange of services. Each party provides help to the other at some point in life. It was not seen as a strict business arrangement—"you give this to me and I will give you something of equal value". There was probably no intent to exact a payback at the time the original service was rendered. It was given freely. And because it was given freely, the second party found it difficult to do less.

Parents had provided for the emotional, social, physical and health needs of their children as they were growing up. The now-grown daughters chose to do the same for their parents who were in need at this point in their lives. A sense of fairness was at play here, but it went beyond a feeling of obligation for a debt incurred. There was a real desire not just to "give back" that which had been given to them, but to demonstrate a value that they had learned from watching their parents make sacrifices to enrich the lives of their loved ones.

Reciprocity.

Georgia realized that her special physical disabilities demanded even more sacrifices from her mother—a single parent. This knowledge increased her desire to "be there" for her mother as she slowly lost the ability to care for others or even herself.

"Well, I wanted to be the caregiver because my mom, she always took care of me as well as she could when I had this Cerebral Palsy. I had fourteen operations, and she was right there when I had all fourteen of them. And looked over me. So that's a big reason too, that I wanted to be a caregiver. If I thought that I could take care of her, I would, you know."

Bernice described this feeling as more of a role-reversal. "I just wanted to make sure that she was all right. You know, it's like I'm the parent now. She's the child, and you want to make sure your child's O.K. That she's being taken care of. And that she doesn't need anything."

For Dorothy the roles could never really be reversed. No matter how much a daughter gives, it can never match that which was given to her. "But, you know, My philosophy on life is—I know I did a lot for my mother. But I tell people that your mother will give more than you will ever give to her. She gave you life."

Beyond reciprocity.

This demonstration of reciprocity is more than quid pro quo. It is the unshakable belief that the parent's love really knows no end, and the daughter's love for her parent runs just as deep. This kind of love inevitably results in an overwhelming desire to give without restraint, knowing that the other *would* do likewise—not because you ask it, but because she could do no less. The following exchange with Evelyn demonstrates her understanding of this kind of love.

Evelyn: *I always felt she lived for me. In fact, people always told me that. (Crying) I remember when I was a kid—I don't know if you've ever seen the Joan Crawford movie, Mildred Pierce. Her cousin used to call her Mildred Pierce. (Crying) Because, you know, I guess she did everything for me. That's whenever that movie was popular. So we used to laugh about that.*

Rick: *So, part of what you're saying here . . . you're not saying the second part, but you're saying, 'She always did things, everything for me, so . . . '*

Evelyn: *She lived for me. She loved me. Very much.*

Rick: *So. . . .*

Evelyn: *I, uh, I loved her very much. We were very close, and I, uh, it was natural to reciprocate.*

Rick: *So there was a reciprocity. 'She did for me. I should do for her.'*

Evelyn: *Yes. It's my turn to do for her. (Crying) Because she would have done the same for me. Had I been sick or ill or whatever.*

Rick: *I haven't had anybody else say that yet. 'She would have done the same thing.' I've had people say the first part. 'She did for me.' But not, 'She would have done the same thing for me.'*

Evelyn: *She would have done the same for me.*

In a later interview, Maureen echoed Evelyn's sentiments more concisely. "My daddy would have done the same thing for me, had he been in good health and I had been the one that was sick. He would have. He would have took care of me."

Factors Relating to Quality of Care

For many caregivers, the decision regarding who should care for the parent was based on the determination of who could provide the best care. Many factors entered into the conclusion of what constituted the "best care". Central to that issue for almost half of the daughters in the study was the belief that keeping their parents as independent as possible for as long they could would result in better quality of life— better quality of care. Thus, their proximity to their parents' houses and their willingness to assume the role in order to enable their parents to remain in their own homes led to them as the inevitable choice as caregivers.

For others, the issue had little to do with independence. It had more to do with the consequences of not providing direct care for their aging parents.

Avoid placement in a nursing home.

Many caregivers had limited knowledge of available options for care. A good number lived in areas where few services were available and the options were, indeed, scarce. When caregivers believed that the only alternative to caring for their parents was to place them in a nursing home, they often decided that there was really no choice but to take on the role, themselves. Nearly half were convinced that the quality of care in a nursing home was poor—that they were, in fact, placing their parents at risk, or that they were betraying their parents and going against their wishes by turning the care over to nursing homes.

Caregivers often expressed very strong feelings about the quality of care one might expect in a long-term care facility. " . . . I couldn't have put her in a home," Evelyn told me. "To me, that's cruel."

Helen also talked about her fears concerning treatment in a nursing home. "I don't think they're good to them in nursing homes. Um, I've worked in them, a few, off and on. You . . . I just seen too much mistreatment."

Dorothy softened the condemnation just a bit. "I had promised her about the nursing home bit. As long as she could walk. Because I had had health problems myself. And I held up to that. Then I knowed in my heart that she wouldn't get the care in a nursing home—which I have nothing against nursing homes. They're a good thing for people that just . . . because everybody just don't have the stamina, sense of humor, whatever it takes to be a caregiver. But I didn't want her in a nursing home. I knowed she wouldn't get the care."

Bernice also made that promise that was so often made by daughters in the study. "She took care of me. You know. And I'm hoping if something happened to me, my son . . . which he won't—he already told me he'd put me in a home (Laughter)—would take care of me. You know, and I always swore to my mother—and I know this is stupid—I always swore to my mother I'd never put her in a home."

Although Flora was able to care for her mother for some time, she eventually found that she was unable to honor her promise to keep her mother out of a nursing home . "Well, I know they . . . they say they get good care, and I believe they do. I have nothing against them, but it's just not . . . you can't be there with them 24 hours. And if Mom gets belligerent with them, you don't know what's going to happen. If she doesn't want to eat, you don't know if they've got the time—or the proper things to feed her. And it was just that my . . . all my life I said—and I sure found out it was different when I got older—I would never see my mother-in-law, because she was as dear to me as my mother, and I always said I would never see her or my mom in a rest home. Look what happened. They both went up there. And I thought, maybe, that I could take care of Mother until she passed away. I really thought I could."

Much of this concern about the quality of care in a nursing home may be unfounded—based on misconceptions and out-dated information. Yet, Maureen's perception of care at nursing homes was based on observation.

Maureen: *We felt like that . . . right . . . I felt that I . . . I knew that I could give him better care than what we had seen. And, uh, well one of my sisters, uh, who had power of attorney for my father, decided we would put him in a . . . she decided we would put him in a, a skilled nursing home, which was in the valley. And that didn't work but two days and nights. We didn't like what we saw. We went there, uh, at eleven o'clock at night. They told us we could come any time we wanted to. We went there and our father's legs were paralyzed.*

Rick: *From what?*

Maureen: *From shots. Because he walked a lot. He walked all the time. They did not want him to, so they put him down with shots. And, uh, he had mind enough really to tell us what had happened. So, um, we decided there and then to ... we didn't want him there. So, we took him out the next day. Brought him to my house.*

Daughter's belief that she can provide best care.

For some daughters it is not a matter of trying to keep parents in their own homes or trying to keep them out of nursing homes. To them it is simply a matter of providing the best care possible, and they believe that they are the most capable providers of that care.

Bernice explains the concern she had over anyone else trying to provide care for her parents. "I just feel . . . I kind of think that I just took them because if I didn't do it, nobody else would. It wouldn't get done. And, of course, the therapist used to say, `But it will.' But I don't think it would. And maybe I don't think it would get done to the ability that I want to see it done—and that I do it. Because I have this thing that . . . the therapist used to say, `Why do you go visit your mother every day? You don't have to do that.' Like he used to give me heck because I would go to the hospital before I left town to visit my brother, when she was at Chestnut Ridge. I used to go up there. And he used to look at the thing and see that I'd signed in there every day. Because you had to sign in. And he'd go, `Why?' I just wanted to make sure that she was all right."

Factors Relating to Sibling Relationships

Family dynamics, in general, are remarkably complex, and they are no less so for the family with a dementia patient. It would be ludicrous to attempt to unravel the interrelationships that exist among siblings in this study. However, the following descriptions demonstrate that they do play a role in the caregiver selection process.

Family just assumed that she would be the caregiver.

So often the daughters described the lack of any conscious decision about how care would be provided for their parents. Sometimes they described a slow evolution, where, inch by inch, they became more the caregiver. Other times, they explained it in more fatalistic terms. There did not seem to be any explanation for how they were selected—beyond mere chance.

Yet, they sometimes described it in terms of a family expectation. Because of circumstances or how they were viewed within the family structure, they were seen by their parents and siblings as the natural choice as caregiver. When the need arose, it was just assumed by all that these daughters would fill the role. It was taken for granted that they would best be able to perform the task and that they would accept the role. And without questioning the process of selection, they did accept it.

The following exchange with Dorothy demonstrates this process.

Rick: *During those early days, when you were trying to decide what to do—um, I'm talking about your extended family now, not your nuclear family—just your extended family. Was there ever any meeting? Or did everybody get together and say, 'Let's decide what to do here. Dorothy should be the caregiver.'? Or was that something that just kind of evolved?*

Dorothy: *. . . . they—I guess they assumed, you know, just like today, if any of them get sick, they're going to call me. You know, and all. And they just assume that I always will be around, which isn't necessarily so.*

In some cases it seems that the entire family was of one mind about the caregiving issue. No decision needed to be made and no discussion was necessary. Words were not even required to express the wishes of the family. There was simply an assumption by all regarding the matter. The selected daughter may have made the same assumption, or she may have simply bowed to the wishes of the others.

Easier to assume role than to fight with sibling.

Some of the daughters who assumed the role of caregiver were not so naive about the subtle manipulation of their siblings. These daughters knew that they were being treated unfairly—that they were being taken advantage of. Still they allowed themselves to be placed in the position. Why? The answer is simple to them.

It simply seemed easier to them to accept the role than to put up the fight that would be required of them to resist. It would exact less energy expenditure. It would not require the fortitude that a major confrontation would demand. It would not take the emotional toll on her that the daily struggle to argue, resist and stand firm would. So, she decided that she would not be worn down, day by day, but rather take on the challenge and get on with her life. As Bernice said about her brother, "Instead of hearing that, it was just simpler to do it and not have to call him and say anything."

Avoid confrontation in asking sibling for help.

It is not uncommon for caregiving daughters to think that they have no right to expect help from their siblings. It is as if they believe that they are shirking their responsibility by making the request. They feel, or are made to feel, that the request is unreasonable and places an unwarranted burden on other family members. Bernice felt guilty for even asking her brothers for help with the caregiving role. She could not completely explain why she should feel guilt, but she felt it just the same.

Bernice: *And then I'd call him and say, 'Can you come up and sit with Mom tonight because I'd like to go to the movie or something with Tom. He'd always, 'Well, I guess, but I was going to do this or I was. . . . ' And then it would make me feel guilty because I asked him.*

Rick: *Does he live in Morgantown?*

Bernice: *Yeah. He lives here.*

Rick: *Lives here in Morgantown . . . you asked him for some help and he said, 'Well, I guess maybe I can come up there.' But it made you feel guilty.*

Bernice: *MmmHmm.*

Rick: *What were you thinking? That you should feel guilty for asking him, but he didn't need to feel guilty for asking you to do the same thing?*

Bernice: *Yeah. I guess so.*

Rick: *Why? What was your thinking? What was your reasoning during that time? That said, 'He should be doing whatever he wants to do, but I have to do this.'*

Bernice: *Uh, I think you have to know my brother to know that he always wants somebody to feel sorry for him. Because, like he works and he really doesn't make all that much where he works, so he does all this work at night. It's like I was taking away from him and his work at night. And he was putting me on the guilt trip for it. And so I felt . . . it got to where I wouldn't ask. That's why I think I got so stressed out, because I just, I refused to ask.*

Rick: *Because it was just easier to do it than to deal with the guilt?*

Bernice: Yeah.

Belief that none of her siblings would provide care.

Whether or not their perception was accurate, the overwhelming majority of those interviewed believed that there was nobody else who would do the job. Brothers and sisters may have existed. They may have lived nearby and had as much time and as many resources available to them as the caregivers. But, in reality or in the minds of the caregiving daughters, they were the only ones who would take on the role.

Two-thirds of the daughters stated this belief directly. The following short statements selected from their explanations demonstrate not only how alike their thinking was on this issue, but how similar the words were that they chose to state their belief.

Amelia: *(Crying softly) There was nobody else that was going to take care of her.*

Flora: *I knew it was up to me. I had no help from anybody.*

Bernice: *I just feel . . . I kind of think that I just took them because if I didn't do it, nobody else would. . . . So there was only me to do it. And I wasn't going to not do it.*

Helen: *So there really wasn't anybody else. . . . Uh, I didn't see where there was any other choice. Because my sister couldn't, and the other ones wouldn't. Um, you know, the grandchildren won't . . .*

Kathleen: *. . . and there wasn't any place for her to go, so I brought her here with me.*

Nellie: *I was there, and there was nobody else to do it.*

Georgia: *Well it just seems like my two sisters didn't want the responsibility, and they felt like they couldn't handle it. . . . So I had to do it. You know. . . . So it just left me.*

Isabel: *(Crying) Because I couldn't get my family to help me. There was none of them would help. . . . They just didn't want to. They could have helped. Some. But they didn't give no help at all.*

Time after time the same phrase is heard. "There was no one else who would do it." There were so many potential caregivers in the large pool of siblings and other relatives who *could* have provided care. Yet, if the perception of these daughters is accurate, they are the only ones who *would*. It is difficult to say whether or not they are correct; regardless, their conviction is unshakable.

Rick: *You said one of the reasons why you were elected is because,*
            'Somebody had to do it, and I guess I was just elected.' Let's come
            back again to 'somebody had to be elected.' But you had six—five
            other brothers and sisters who could have been elected, too. I want
            to try to get at 'why you' still some more. Would any of them have
            accepted the position like you did if they had been elected?
Dorothy: *No. . . . Speaking of my brothers and sisters, knowing them as I*
            know them. Because, in my heart, and they would tell you, not one
            of them would have done what I did.

External Locus of Control Factors

Most of the women in the study expressed, to some degree, the belief that their selection as caregiver was really beyond their control. A variety of external factors, acting independently or in concert, made their selection inevitable or, at least, greatly increased the likelihood that they would end up with the caregiving role.

The decision of who would be caregiver seemed to them to be in the hands of others or dependent on the whims of the gods. There was little or nothing that these daughters could do to control the course of events that led to their assumption of the role. The following are some of the forces that the women in the study believed to be controlling or influencing their selection as caregiver.

Patient decided.

Some of the adult women in the study appeared to retain the earlier parent-child relationship that they had experienced in their youth, when their mothers or fathers made decisions for them and they simply acquiesced. There was no questioning here. The parents' wishes were seen less as desires and more as statements of how things would be.

It did not appear to matter what the parents' decisions were based on or whether their desires matched those of their daughters. Once their wants were made known, there was no further discussion; the issue was settled.

There was no arguing about the decision. There was no attempt to influence it. There seemed to be no resentment toward the parents or the siblings. Perhaps because the daughters were flattered to be the chosen ones, or maybe because the family dynamics exacted compliance—whatever the reason, the selection was perceived as being outside their control, and the daughters assumed the role of caregiver.

Georgia described this as succinctly as any of the caregivers.

Georgia: *Well, then I, I . . . well, she kind of made the decision. She told me that she wanted my . . . her oldest granddaughter, my niece, to come in and help, because she couldn't remember how to spell the words to write out the checks and stuff. So the oldest granddaughter came in and helped her for quite awhile, before . . . you know. Then one day she told me, 'I want you to take over.' She said, 'I can't handle this responsibility anymore.' She said, 'I can't remember.' So I took over.*

Rick: *So you took over the household.*

Georgia: *Yes.*

Rick: *The business of the household and taking care of her?*

Georgia: *Her, yeah.*

Georgia has two sisters, one brother, and several nieces and nephews (her mother's grandchildren). Regardless, her mother had made her wishes known and, thus, the selection was made.

Isabel voices the same sentiments about her willingness to abide by her parents' wishes. She does so with a hint of pride that she was chosen above the others.

Rick: *. . . . why were you the one selected?*

Isabel: *Because they thought that they could trust me.*

Rick: *They thought that they could trust you?*

Isabel: *Yeah. Dad and Mom said they knew they could trust me. Dad said, Dad always said, 'You're my number one.'*

Rick: *They could count on you?*

Isabel: *Yep. I was always there for them.*

While the parent may have made the choice in some families, it was sometimes at the prompting of others. Bernice's mother lived just down the road from her. When her mother's behaviors started getting worrisome, Bernice's brother came in from out of state and took her home for a week. At the end of the week, he was convinced that she could no longer stay on her own.

Bernice: . . . . *I think he made his wife explain to my mother that she had three choices. Well, she kind of explained to my mom about the disease and everything, and that she really couldn't stay by herself . . . I mean, totally. And my brother told her she had three choices: she could stay with any one of us three kids. Any one of us would take her. She could have somebody come in the house . . . or she could go to a nursing home. 'These are your choices. You have to pick one before I take you back home.'*

Not surprisingly, she chose to return home and Bernice and a part-time paid caregiver shared responsibility for her care.

Another family member decided.

This last excerpt could be interpreted as the patient deciding, but it could just as easily be seen as another family member making the decision. Given the ultimatums presented by the brother, it was probably fairly clear what the mother's choice would be.

When another family member makes the decision regarding caregiving, it is often done more subtly than when the parents, alone, express their desires.

Dorothy: *Well, you know, personally, my theory on that was—out of sight, out of mind. I think. And I think, I don't care how many children there is, I think there's going to be one do the most of it. I think there's going to be one to do the biggest majority, you know. And, uh, so they just left it up to me, you know. . . . Well, somebody had to do the job, so I guess I was elected.*

Helen's sister and brother-n-law were a bit more direct. Helen had a choice. It is just that her options were somewhat limited.

Helen: *They were going to put her in a rest home, my sister was, and, uh, said either come and get her or they'll put her in a rest home . . .*

Rick: *And he kind of gave you an ultimatum. 'Come and get her or I'll put her in a rest home.'*

Helen: *Right. Right.*

Siblings, in-laws—even the non-demented parent can make the decision or, at least influence it. Laura's father was dying of cancer and Laura was providing care for him.

Rick: *You kind of fell into the role of helping take care of your dad, so it*
         was just a natural thing. . . .
Laura: *To move in to take care of my mother. Right. I also think, too—and I*
         can't really say that I ever actually remember an eyeball-to-eyeball
         exchange with my father—but I actually think that he was grooming
         me and was approaching me or appealing to me to reassure him that
         I would take care of her (Laura's mother with dementia). That this
         would continue.

Role evolved slowly over time.

Jackie dropped everything to come to her mother's aid. She did not, however, realize that she would be devoting her life to the care of her mother. She saw her role as a manager of services—a long distance manager, at that. She was surprised when things did not work out that way.

Jackie: *Because I really didn't think it was going to take this much time. I*
         figured that I would come to West Virginia, get Mamma some in-
         home help . . . so my thing was I'd go there, get Mamma set up with
         some services, then I'd go on about my business. But once I got
         there, I couldn't do that.

It was not easy finding the services that her mother needed. Those that she did find were expensive, and the procedures required to receive financial assistance were complex and time-consuming. What at first appeared to be a temporary situation for Jackie now looks as if it could become an all-consuming, life-long role.

The same kind of situation was described by Evelyn. There was no single point at which she realized that she had taken on the caregiving role. She began by performing one task and then added another and another. Before she knew it, she was the primary caregiver. She may not have decided any differently if she had been given the choice up-front. But that is not the way it happened.

"Well, I don't know as I was a choice. (Laughter) I was just there, and I was the only one. You know, it evolved, I guess. I, I used to think that I had no grip or control over my life during that time."

Dorothy too watched the caregiving role evolve. For her, it began very early in life, long before her mother developed dementia.

"Uh, I was the last to get married of the group. I took care of my mother. I took care of my baby sister. She lived with my mother. I worked. My mother and I did. So I sort of . . . like when my husband and I got married, we—like he said, he inherited her. You know. And people would say, `How long have you had her?' All my life".

The role evolved from giving financial and emotional support to a healthy single parent to Dorothy providing total care in her home for her mother. Over a period of years, her mother's needs progressed from minor assistance to total custody. Her life ended in a vegetative state with Dorothy spending hours each day using an eyedropper to try to get enough fluids and nutrition in her to keep her alive.

Natural, normal part of the life cycle.

Some caregivers do not see the role or this time in their lives as being so special. It is simply a different experience—perhaps more difficult in some ways, but still just one more episode in a life filled with joys and burdens. It was simply there for them to do, and they did it. "You do what you have to do. That's what I've always done, you know," Nellie said in a voice that was weary but perfectly accepting of what life had to offer.

It is just part of life's cycle—one of life's many tasks. Some things are handed to one person, others to another. We do not choose what gets handed to us; our task is just to see that it gets done.

Dorothy said it this way. "I had a job, and I did it. And my job is over, so . . . it's just like anything. It's just a part of your life. So, you pick up and go on from there. You know. So that part's back. So you go on to this and this and this."

Religious reasons.

Some women believe that their selection was completely outside their control; a few believe that it was in the hands of a Higher Being. Either through God's teachings or through His direct intervention, these women were guided to this role. For some, this is an act of atonement, for others a blessing, and for a few it is an opportunity to express God's love through them.

"Well, it's the Christian thing to do, for one thing," Opal told me in response to my question.

Maureen echoed Opal's sentiments:

Maureen: Well, um, the Bible says, `Do unto others as you would have them do unto you.' And I think people—if they would take the Word for what is says—I think God expects us to take care of our own. I've always been taught that way. And I am a Christian. And I believe in putting the Lord first in my life. And I've had a good life, and I have no regrets for being, for doing what I could do. I just wish I'd have done more.

Not all of the women were happy with God's intervention or with their religious upbringing. Laura has left the Church but her beliefs are still influenced by its teachings. With sarcastic humor that underscores a certain amount of bitterness, she explained the role that religion played in her selection.

Laura: I think it's probably good for me to do this as kind of little—this is Papal retentive—to have to do this thing because of the Catholic background in my background. That I may be doing penance for having been such a pain in Carie's (her mother) side, such a thorn in her side all these years. That I will now get the assignment of penance. O.K., you know, like thirty Hail Marys and two days in Purgatory. That's right—Purgatory.

For Jackie, this picture is not quite so clear. She is still thinking through the whole matter of Divine Intervention. She has no doubts, however, that it did play some role.

Jackie: . . . And it was like . . . I didn't have control. I mean, period. I came to do that. Looky here. I came here with my mom going crazy. . . . It's so amazing. I had went to church. I always go to church. That's my thing. That's my thing, O.K.? But I was in church and I said, "Lord, I told you to order my steps." I mean, I didn't know what direction I was going to go. Or where I was needed. I really didn't. But at the same time, here I am, utilizing every part of me, right?

Unable to complete her thoughts on this topic, Jackie left this discussion unfinished, only to return to it later in the interview.

Jackie: .... *"Why did I do this?" Other than being, I think, called to do it. And I believe. ...*

Rick: *Being called?*

Jackie: *By whatever, you know. You know what?*

Rick: *I just want to make sure I understand. I'm sure I do, but I just want to ... you're saying that maybe that God ... that this is part of God's plan.*

Jackie: *Spiritually. Yeah. ... [I had just been out to see Mom.] And I was on my way back to California, O.K.? On the airplane. When I was a young girl, there was this lady named Miss Donner. She was an old lady—in fact, I mentioned her earlier—whose house my mom bought. And so I used to go over and comb her hair. And I'd talk to her. And those are the people who nurtured me. See? People say, `Oh, your mom prayed for you.' My mom never prayed for me. I learned the Bible from an old blind lady who used to read me the Bible out of Braille, O.K.? She had a Braille Bible. And we used to sit at her legs and she'd read us stories. But Miss Donner told me when I was crying one day. Because Mamma had been really mean or whatever, and I'd go sit and talk to Miss Donner. And I was crying. And Miss Donner said, she said, `Well, Baby.' She said, `You know how your mamma is to your brother and sister.' And she said, `But one day she's going to need you. One day you'll be the one that'll take care of her.' And then, this is the Gospel truth, O.K.? Miss Donner died, oh, after I left West Virginia. Let's see, I've been out of the house about twenty-five years. So, I guess she's been dead about that time—about twenty-six, twenty-seven years. O.K. Now I'm coming back on the plane from here, going to California. And Miss Donner said the same thing. In my mind. I mean, I'm up in the air, right? And I mean, this lady that I haven't talked to in twenty, thirty years— she says, `You know, it's time for you to go take care of your mom.' And I heard the whole conversation. In my head, O.K.? And so, when I came back to California, it was like it was set. O.K.? It was like it was set. There was Miss Donner telling me, `It's time for you to take care of your mamma.' Simple.*

An accident, purely chance.

Some of the caregivers truly believed that they fell into the role for no particular reason. It could have happened to anybody. They just happened to be in the right place (or the wrong place) at the right time.

"If my sister had came back and seen Mom first, she maybe would have become the caregiver. I think it's who. . . . I stepped into a can of worms. And once you step into that can of worms, you can't. . . . It's like mud, like quicksand."

In the minds of these daughters, it was just a matter of the luck of the draw. It could have happened to any of their brothers or sisters just as easily. It just happens that they drew the short straw.

Factors That Benefit The Caregiver

For most of the women in the study, providing care for their parents was viewed as an act of giving. Yet, many of the caregivers realized that they too were receiving something from the experience. They spoke of ways in which they had been rewarded for the work, positive feelings that they had experienced, and new perspectives that they had gained. These seemed to be side effects—often unanticipated—to the act of giving.

In addition to this group, were women who described these "caregiver benefits" not as side effects, but as part of their reason for providing care. They stated this without the slightest hint of guilt. They believed that it was perfectly acceptable to perform the task, in part, because of the rewards that it held.

Financial incentive.

Only one caregiver mentioned money as a motivation for taking care of her mother. While she discussed seven others factors that she believed led to her acceptance of the role of caregiver, she was quite clear in stating that money played a part in the decision.

It should be pointed out that she was not describing a wealth of assets to which she would gain access. Rather, the two appeared to live at or near the poverty level in a one-room trailer, curtained off to create two bedrooms and a kitchen/living room area. The money that she spoke about was vaguely referred to as a "government check".

Helen: . . . . *Uh, no, I didn't have to bring her here, but, uh, I feel she's better off. And I'm better off keeping a home, because I do keep the home. It don't look like it, but I do. And her money comes here and . . . so that, you know. She still keeps the home.*

Rick: *[After a number of other factors were mentioned in a rather lengthy discussion.] O.K. You said a third thing there. Let me just see if I can pull it out of my memory. . . .*

Helen: *Money? (Laughter)*

Rick: *Well, yeah, you did say money, too. And we'll come back to that in a few seconds. [After further discussion was held concerning other factors.] Let me come back to the other point that you made earlier. You said, `Money.' Now what do you mean by that?*

Helen: *Well, I wasn't working. So, her income comes into the house. And, uh, so that's what I mean by `money'. Because God knows, I didn't get any money from mom—my dad or her.*

Rick: *But you're able to share in the household here—in the living expenses and stuff. You're able to share in that.*

Helen: *Who? Me and my mother?*

Rick: *You both get to. . . .*

Helen: *Well, sure, she gets the, uh, she gets $xxx a month. And I get $xxx. Yes, it all goes into the house. And, uh. . . .*

Rick: *So, that makes it easier when you're sharing living expenses. Makes it easier. That's what you're saying.*

Helen: *Yeah. Well, I think she carries the whole thing, because [my] $xxx a month's nothing. You know, what's that? Buy me a pack of cigarettes and a coffee once in awhile. (Laughter)*

Recognition

There is a certain amount of acknowledgment on the part of those surrounding the caregiver regarding the hard work involved in the role and the special qualities required to perform it. Sometimes this recognition is expressed openly; other times it is perceived by the caregiver without the need for verbalization. While they may prefer the help of family and friends rather than this grudging admiration, they do get a sense that this is some compensation for their sacrifice.

Dorothy: . . . . *But, uh, they don't understand how I did it. If you would interview any of them, they'd say that they couldn't have done it. I*

> *mean, you can get on the phone and call any of them. They'd say,*
> *'We don't know how she did it. We couldn't do it.'*

Dorothy says this with a great deal of pride. It is well-deserved praise, and she has a right to glory in the moment. At first glance it would appear that this is a response to be expected—this bit of basking in the limelight. There is, however, something about the way that she says it, something about the way that she acts as she tells the story that suggests that this goes beyond the scope of side benefit and may be one of the factors that motivated her to accept and maintain the role.

SUMMARY

It is obvious that the above-mentioned categories are not entirely clear-cut. It could be argued that some of the factors identified could fit as well in one category as the next. It could even be the case that the same factor given by two different caregivers might best be placed in separate categories because of the contextual nature of their individual stories. The structuring of the 38 factors into categories should be seen as an attempt to organize cumbersome data rather than a definitive classification that exists in the real world. The 38 factors are the stories of the women in the study; the 10 categories comprise a structure that comes from my interpretation of those stories.

These stories lose a great deal when individual factors are simply culled to produce a list. The continuity of the tale, the context of caregiver statements, the sense of 'lived experiences' is lost, to a great extent. A picture of caregiver selection begins to emerge, but it does so at the expense of individual portraits of fifteen remarkable women.

While it is not possible to recount their stories verbatim, a fuller picture will be presented in the next chapter. Impressions were gained from reading between the lines, from hearing what was not said as well as what was, from having the benefit of a shared experience with these women that goes beyond a written transcript, and from having the opportunity to hold pieces of fifteen lives simultaneously in my mind.

The insights gained provide still another picture of caregiving daughters and the process by which they came to provide for the well-being of their parents. It is the cumulative effect of these various views (stated reasons, categories, themes, caregivers' perceptions, interviewer's interpretations) that helps creates a realistic image of these women that goes beyond the one-dimensional representation that any of them singly can provide.

CHAPTER V

Discussion

Patterns that were identified and the theoretical framework that was developed will be presented in this chapter. This will be followed by a discussion of the potential impact of the study and implications of the findings. Finally, limitations of the study and implications for further research will be presented.

PATTERNS

The women interviewed for this study are unique—different from that segment of society who have not been caregivers, but also quite distinct within their own group. Once one has spent time with Dorothy, it would be difficult to confuse her with Jackie, Opal, or Bernice. With little practice it would be possible to listen to an individual statement pulled from the transcripts and correctly identify the speaker. These women have their own stories; there is no such thing as *the* caregiver.

There are, however, commonalties—similar perspectives among some, parallel experiences among others. The daughters often made statements that sounded much like those of others in the group, and described the situations in which they found themselves in terms that closely resembled those of their fellow-caregivers.

As the interviews progressed, certain patterns began to emerge. The term *pattern*, here, is not defined as the mere repetition of phrases found in the interview transcripts. The same "reason" for becoming a caregiver was often given by more than one woman in the study. Those repeated statements may have warranted the creation of a new "category". However, that collection of identical or nearly identical reasons should not be confused with the patterns that exist in the narratives of the caregivers.

Rather, patterns are underlying connecting threads that run throughout the interviews. They are inferences rather than caregiver statements. It is their shared meaning that gives them an identity and their recurrence that gives them significance. They provide insights that help to produce an understanding that surpasses that provided by the "raw data".

They are interpretations. They are neither the words nor the thoughts of the caregivers in the study. They are deductions or conclusions that I have reached, not by hypothesis-testing but by allowing my intuitive nature to balance my more developed rational side.

Nonetheless, to be included here, there had to be adequate support for them within the stories of the daughters, either through their direct statements and actions or the implications of those expressions. If they could not be substantiated, they would be of little more value than a guess.

I did discard some potential patterns as being insupportable. Yet, while I was convinced that the remaining patterns had substance, I was still troubled. Some of them seemed at odds with direct statements made by the caregivers. For instance, caregivers described the numerous ways in which they were abandoned by their siblings. Yet, it seemed to me that some were quite concerned that their brothers and sisters not be judged harshly. Others explained, early on, the burdens and hardships that they had to endure in the caregiving role. Later, however, I sensed their need to describe the same events in a much more positive light, downplaying the negative side of the experience. I was clearly receiving two messages. Did that mean that one was right and the other wrong?

Having given much thought to the matter and still believing in both the caregiver statements and my impressions, I began to search for some explanation that could meld the two. Was it possible that they could be antithetical and yet compatible? If so, could the combination of the two bring deeper understanding of the forces at work in the process of caregiver selection?

DIFFICULTIES IN RESPONDING

For some of the daughters, the question of caregiver selection was difficult to contemplate. They do not typically think in terms of cause and effect. They wrestle with more concrete and practical questions in their lives. It is difficult for them to consider their own motivations or those of their siblings. They acknowledge that external forces influence their lives, but have little interest or practice in considering what they are or how they function.

Others had no problem with the difficulty of the question, but rather its seeming simplicity. They had trouble getting beyond the obvious. Their parents needed care, so they provided it. One daughter stated that it was like the question posed to Willy Sutton, the notorious bank robber, in an attempt to understand his anti-social behavior. "Why do I rob banks? Because that's where the money is."

For many caregivers, the challenge of responding to the query is in attempting to recall the moment when they took on the role of provider. Often times, there is not a single point in time when the caregiving role was accepted. It is hard to remember "how" when they do not even recall "when". They never made a clear, conscious decision to become caregivers. There was no family meeting, where all concerned came together to decide how care would be provided for Mom or Dad. Rather, the situation just seemed to evolve slowly over time, and the daughters emerged as the caregivers.

In order to understand how they came to the role, daughters would have to go back in their minds to a time prior to assuming the position. As stated earlier, I stumbled across the implications of this insight by accident. In an attempt to relax the subjects on the first interview, I spent a good deal of time engaging them in casual conversation. When I believed that they were ready to begin the formal ("real") interview, I would ask a question that was meant to be a transition between chit-chat and data collection: Would you tell me something about what your parent was like before the dementia and how you came to recognize that care was needed?

The question was meant to encourage them to begin thinking about the broad issue of dementia and caregiving. It was not intended to elicit any data about the caregiving decision. Inevitably, the daughters found it almost impossible to pinpoint specific episodes or points in time when they knew for certain that their parents had dementia. Almost from the beginning of the interviews, it became clear that the ambiguity surrounding the recognition of the onset of dementia was tied closely to the uncertainty about the process of her acceptance of the role.

Just as there was no single point in time when caregivers recalled accepting the position, there was no single decision that they made to do so. It was a series of smaller decisions that surreptitiously added up to the big one.

They decided to question their parents' ability to function as well as they once had. They decided to check on them occasionally and help out with small everyday tasks that seemed to be troublesome. They determined that their parents were reaching the point where their safety was compromised and some sort of intervention would be required.

They did not know where these and other decisions were leading them. They were taking one step at a time, not even suspecting that another step would follow. Yet, each step moved them closer to their destination, and they were surprised one day when they heard themselves being referred to as caregivers.

The term was probably first heard with their initial contact with the formal health care system. It almost certainly was not heard from a family member. Families in the study tended to hold remarkably little discussion about any aspect of care.

Especially in the days before care was perceived as needed, the topic seems to be as much of a conversational taboo as death, itself. Families avoided talking openly about it. When daughters in the study were asked what their siblings thought about the provision of care during this period, they simply could not say. There had been no discussion about it.

Not only had there been little or no talk about caregiving, there was scant thought given to it, at least on the part of the daughters. Almost none had, at any earlier point in her life, imagined a time when her parents might need this type of help. They had seen other older adults who had become frail and dependent. Some had even known elders with dementia. Yet, somehow, the idea that this could happen in their families eluded them. The few families who had vaguely anticipated the possibility of some future need for care made no concrete plans about how that care would be provided.

With the gradual evolution of the role and little prior thought or talk about it, it is no wonder that the daughters had such a difficult time responding to the question of how they had become caregivers. At first glance, it is puzzling to imagine how these women could fail to contemplate the possibility of accepting the caregiving role at some time in their lives. It is so common today that it seems almost inevitable that everyone will be faced with such decisions.

However, it must be remembered that this is really a pioneer generation in caregiving. It is not the case that caregivers were non-existent before this generation, but society had not seen caregivers in these numbers prior to this. Life expectancy of aging parents exonerated most adult children.

There was little, then, to prepare these women for what they would face. The warning signs were not as visible as they are today. There were not the constant reminders. And there were few role models to show them how it could be done—how the decision could be made and how the care could be provided.

LACK OF KNOWLEDGE

This relative paucity of caregiving role models seems to have had an impact on several aspects of the lives of the women in the study. They have had to assume the role unprepared in many ways.

There appears to be an almost complete lack of awareness, on their part, of care options. For many, the question they asked themselves was simply, "Do we put Mom in a nursing home, or do I take her in?" There is little evidence of any consideration of shared care, in-home care provided by non-profit, profit, or volunteer agencies, or full-time paid care.

They seem to have had almost as little knowledge in the beginning about the disease—its diagnosis, symptoms, progression, or treatment. They had little idea how to best interact with someone with dementia and were at a complete loss as to what the caregiving role would entail or how to provide the best care.

There often seems to be a lack of awareness of how actions and decisions early in life impact the circumstances in which they find themselves later. For instance, it seems possible that some caregivers unwittingly positioned themselves psychologically, socially, and geographically for the role well before there was any need for care.

This is most clearly seen in the daughter who remained at home (in or near the family "homeplace") while her siblings moved away in young adulthood. She often sacrificed her opportunity for a career or a family of her own to do so. She stayed near her parents geographically and psychologically throughout her youth and middle age. She retained an important place in their social world. In time, she became the overwhelming favorite and logical choice as caregiver.

There is nothing inappropriate about her decision to stay, just as there is nothing wrong with her acceptance of the role of caregiver. If there is anything troublesome here, it is her apparent inability to see the consequences of these early decisions.

I truly believe that this positioning takes place. I am less certain about the level of awareness surrounding it. The daughters appear to be rather naive about the subtle process. Do they position themselves unconsciously or is there some intent on their part?

It is possible that they are placed in this position by their parents. Is it that one of the children is chosen early on and, through socialization within the family, learns to position herself so?

While there is no hard evidence of this, there is some interesting demographic information on the subjects. In this study, ten of the fifteen women were either the eldest or youngest child, perhaps a natural position for "the chosen one".

There was no attempt at random statistical sampling in this study, and the numbers are much too small for any sort of generalizability. Yet, the pattern is intriguing and does cause one to wonder.

A number of patterns suggest a lack of awareness or knowledge about some aspect of the role of caregiving. At times, the caregivers in the study would request information about the disease or want to know about norms in caregiving. The information was given to them or they were referred to appropriate resource persons.

One interesting pattern emerged concerning the lack of awareness of caregivers regarding their selection. The level of understanding rose with the mere asking of the question. For many, it was a question never consciously contemplated before, and perhaps intentionally avoided. Time and again, the daughters marveled at the insights that they gained while trying to respond to my question.

They had spent years in the role, and it remained a mystery. Yet, the simple asking of a question opened a floodgate of thoughts and understanding for some.

Of course, the doors that were opened brought along with understanding a deluge of tears and painful memories for many. Yet, they found the interviews to be bittersweet affairs, for they had a healing effect, as well. Almost all expressed thanks for the "therapeutic" experience.

The fact of the matter is that most of the caregivers have no opportunity to talk to anyone about what they have gone through. The have kept bottled up inside them their frustrations, fears, heartaches, and concerns. They have had no one to ask questions of and no one to give answers to. While it may be healthy to verbally express one's feelings, it is difficult to have a dialogue with oneself. For lack of a confidant, many simply went through the years without questioning.

COMPLEXITY OF THE ISSUE

Once the daughters were encouraged to think about the issue of how they had become caregivers, once they were given the opportunity to talk about it, they realized that it was a far more complex matter than they had imagined. At the same time, I, too, began to understand that I had underestimated its complexity.

Subjects typically began by giving a single reason as *the* reason for their selection. It was as if this were a test. I had asked a question; they were to give me the answer. One subject actually asked what would happen if she gave me the wrong answer.

There were often long, awkward pauses after their first response. They felt that they had answered my question and seemed to be wondering what they were to do next and how we were going to fill the hours to come.

As I struggled with ways to get them to expand on their original statements and tried to think of different ways to ask the same question, they sometimes lost patience, explaining with some exasperation that they had already answered that question.

With a great deal of effort on their part and mine, we did discover that additional reasons emerged as the interviews progressed. These later explanations were often seen by them as being more important and more accurate than the original reason given. They appeared to be new and somewhat surprising insights for the daughters.

A clear insight came to me also at this time. Thinking back to the original design that I had conceptualized to study this question and recalling the literature that I had read where investigators had asked this question as an aside to other caregiver issues, I saw for the first time the danger of asking subjects to respond "off the top of their heads".

Subjects are often given seconds or minutes to respond to rather deep questions about their lives on printed questionnaires. Even in face-to-face interviews, it is difficult to allow or encourage individuals to spend more than a fraction of an hour of contemplation.

The danger here is that the investigator may well end up with rather superficial answers to complex issues. Researchers would not think of writing the discussion section of their research papers without poring over the data for days on end. Yet, we sometimes use data that are the results of little more than a few seconds thought.

I learned much about this process as the interviews progressed. Two short interviews are often better than one long one. Three are better still. Long pauses may be deadly in conversations, but they can be healthy in interviews. As I gained these and other insights, I modified my interview format.

I would ask questions and let them tell me their story. Then I would come back later in the session (or in a follow-up session) and ask the same questions and let them tell me the story again. They typically disclosed more the second time, either by adding to the story or describing events and feelings in a different way.

Sometimes I would let them tell their story and then take a single aspect that they had described and ask them to focus only on that for elaboration. When they were focused on telling the whole story, they tended to summarize, cutting things short in order to get on to the next point.

I also learned that when I interrupted their story for clarification on some point of confusion, they had a difficult time going back to pick up the thread of thought. I learned to hold my tongue and let them lead the way—a difficult lesson for investigators who are more comfortable when they are in control.

I came to believe that follow-up sessions are invaluable for real understanding. It was here that I was able to get them to focus on one thing and to flesh that out as much as possible—exhaust the subject— with no thought as to where we would go next.

Finally, these follow-up sessions gave the daughters time and permission to reflect. Some, anticipating my return, worked at this during the time between visits. Others related that they made no attempt to further consider the matter, but found thoughts just floating in and out of their minds in the intervening days.

As multiple explanations emerged, another pattern came to light. Single reasons were not as simple as they appeared at first glance. They were often inextricably intertwined with others reasons put forward or with reasons left unstated.

Proximity is a good example of this phenomenon. Daughters in the study often gave this as one of the primary reasons for the caregiving role falling to them. They simply lived closest to their parents, and so it only made sense that they would assume the role.

However, proximity, in itself, may not be the sole determining factor. The reason that the daughter lives close-by may be, in part, due to the close relationship between mother and daughter. Thus, the simple answer proximity may involve other factors such as love, feelings of responsibility, or need for parents' approval. There may be the desire to keep parents as independent as possible in the familiar surroundings of their own home, coupled with the knowledge that this can only work if a caregiver lives close by to fill in the gaps in self-care.

Beyond the entwined relationship of two or more stated reasons is the enmeshment of unspoken factors. For example, regardless of closeness of the relationship between adult children and their parents, moving away for twenty or more years is bound to limit contact and, thus, alter that relationship in some ways. This lessened familiarity and subtle change in relationship may have as much to do with distant children being overlooked as caregivers as close proximity has to do with the near daughter being selected for the role.

CONFUSING DATA

Perhaps because of the intertwining of factors and because somewhat opposing reasons were given by the same caregiver at different times over the interview process, the data sometimes seemed to be confusing, if not totally contradictory.

A good example of this is in the way in which the caregivers described their siblings and the role that they played in the care of the parents. Over the course of time, their descriptions changed. Early in the interviews the siblings were sometimes described in somewhat negative terms or, at least, as being of little assistance.

Of course, many of the daughters in the study resented the lack of assistance they received from their siblings. Yet, the animosity that they felt toward their brothers and sisters who did not help or visit seemed to be only partly based on the burden that it placed on them.

To a large extent, the caregivers' anger appeared to be a result of the lack of love for the parent that this behavior demonstrated. They were outraged on their parents' behalf. They seemed to be saying, "You're not just deserting me, but forsaking our mother and father, as well." The daughters' own abandonment may have been tolerable, but their siblings' rejection of their parents was not.

It also became clear that sibling support, or lack thereof, was not limited to physical assistance. In fact, more often than not the emotional support—visits, phone calls, heart-to-heart talks—were viewed as more important than helping with everyday chores.

If their siblings would listen to them when they needed to vent their frustrations and anger, if they would care enough to try to understand what their sisters were going through, if they would express appreciation for what they were doing, the caregivers felt that they were not alone, and they were very gracious in sharing the credit for the care of their parents.

All too often, though, this was not the case. Siblings seemed to distance themselves emotionally as well as physically from their parents and the caregivers.

The daughters saw the injustice of the situation. In tears of futility some related their frustration in trying to learn "the man's job" of fixing a furnace or car when she had a brother who could have performed the task. They spoke of the humiliation that they experienced when first confronted with bathing their fathers—a task they believed more fitting for sons.

Later, however, a different picture of brothers and sisters was painted by caregivers. The same siblings who were earlier castigated were now depicted as contributing in small ways, and supportive when they were not able to help directly. Behaviors that were previously criticized by the daughters were now excused.

There appeared to be a protective nature or attitude on the part of the caregivers that had developed somewhat unexpectedly. When I would question the seeming contradiction, some of the caregivers explained that I had misinterpreted early statements. Others became slightly defensive.

There was a definite change in attitude regarding siblings. It seemed important to the daughters to give the impression that all was well and that the family had worked together to see that the parents were cared for.

At this point, the stories seemed somewhat confusing to me, although the caregivers seemed to feel little conflict. It was not until I had the opportunity to reflect on what the daughters were saying that I began to see how this all fell in place. The shifting views that the daughters held of their siblings helped me to see a broader picture of the whole issue of caregiver selection.

LOGIC VERSUS EMOTION

The selection process was turning out to be very different from the one I would have designed if it had been left to me. As much as I would prefer this to be a purely logical decision on the part of the caregivers, my rational nature could not eliminate the emotional forces at work in their lives.

Neither could it negate the impact of external forces. For instance, the attitude of the husbands of married daughters had to be considered before they could decide to accept the role.

Emotions, family dynamics, societal pressures and a host of other less-than-tidy forces were combining to make chaos out of the neatly-ordered structure that I was hoping to discover. I was left with the prospect of accepting the conclusion that there was no order to all of this, or finding some connection that linked this conflicting data in some way.

THEORETICAL FRAMEWORK

While the individual tales of the daughters in the study and the thirty-eight distinct reasons given by them provide much information to help gain an understanding of the complex process that led to the daughters' selection as caregivers, they do not tell the entire story.

As stated in Chapter III, the purpose of this study is to better understand what factors influence the selection of adult daughters as primary caregivers of parents with dementia. It is important, therefore, to hear what daughters have to say about the determining factors that they have perceived. It is equally important to try to gain additional insight into the process that led to that complex decision.

Because of the methodology chosen for this study, both the identification of the factors and the understanding of the process are based, in large part, on the daughters' ability to grasp the intricacies of the selection process. Therefore, in addition to gaining knowledge about the factors and process, it is imperative that we consider the degree to which the daughters comprehend the forces which have helped shape their selection as caregivers.

My contemplation of discussions with the 15 women in this study has convinced me that the level of understanding varies from daughter to daughter. It has also led me to believe that their comprehension of the mechanisms at work grows over time. It would appear that progress in understanding falls into separate and distinct phases, each building on the one before. While all seem to start at the same point—which I describe as phase one—two paths diverge and lead to entirely different destinations.

What follows is a theory of how this phenomenon unfolds. It is not a hypothesis of how the daughters became caregivers, but rather how they developed in their understanding of that process. It helps to explain the apparent inconsistencies in caregiver statements. It clarifies some of the confusion surrounding changes in caregiver perceptions over time. It links the statements of the daughters with the sometimes conflicting observations of the investigator.

Overview of the Theory

There appears to be a process that caregiving daughters may go through in reaching an understanding of their role and how they acquired it. Their perceptions of how they came to be in their present situation seem to change slowly over time. Both this succession of levels of understanding and this forward progress which builds on previous levels of comprehension lead to consideration of a stage theory to explain this process.

All stage theories have certain inherent problems. They are prone to gross generalization. That which may apply to many is often taken to apply to all. In order to make the theory apply to the masses, there is tendency to make some square pegs fit into round holes.

There is also the danger of taking what was meant as a description of what may be and turning it into a prescription of what should be. Followers of the theory see it not so much as an aid in understanding a complex phenomenon as a course of action along which they need to help their clients move.

Finally, while phases may appear to be distinct on paper, in reality, there is generally much overlap between them. Also, few individuals move strictly in one direction. There is often a good deal of movement back and forth between stages.

There are five levels of understanding in the model being proposed. All begin in phase one with a minimal degree of understanding. From here, caregivers move along one of two tracks, the A-Track leading more quickly toward understanding and ultimately arriving at a higher level of awareness than the B-Track. Phase two is a rather superficial level of understanding for both tracks. By phase three, however, those on the A-Track are leaving their counterparts well behind, both in effort put forth and understanding gained. Little progress is seen by either group in stage four. Most in the B-Track will remain stuck here, with a much larger proportion of the A-Track caregivers reaching some ultimate resolution concerning their role. The diagram on the following page provides a visual representation of the model, while the narrative that follows furnishes a detailed explanation of each phase.

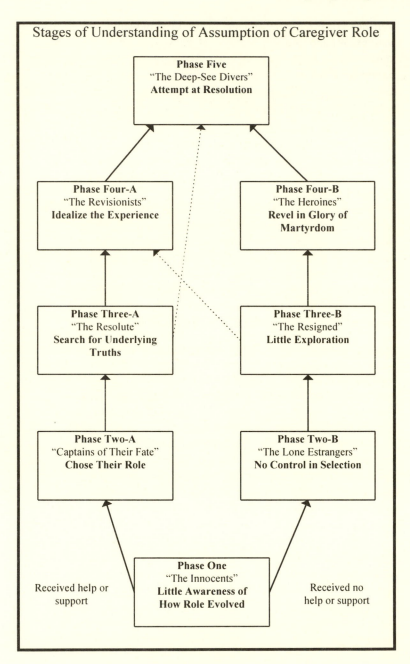

Stages of Understanding of Assumption of Caregiver Role

Phase Five
"The Deep-See Divers"
Attempt at Resolution

Phase Four-A
"The Revisionists"
Idealize the Experience

Phase Four-B
"The Heroines"
Revel in Glory of Martyrdom

Phase Three-A
"The Resolute"
Search for Underlying Truths

Phase Three-B
"The Resigned"
Little Exploration

Phase Two-A
"Captains of Their Fate"
Chose Their Role

Phase Two-B
"The Lone Estrangers"
No Control in Selection

Received help or support

Phase One
"The Innocents"
Little Awareness of How Role Evolved

Received no help or support

Phase One: The Innocents

In this initial stage, caregivers are unable to give an explanation for how they received their role. It is not that they are unwilling to explain; neither is it an inability to articulate that which they understand in their own minds. There is simply little awareness of, and little thought given to, how it came to be.

Few have the time nor energy at this stage for contemplation. Most are in the first months of caregiving, and there is precious little time to devote to musings of anything but the practical. They are overwhelmed by the task at hand. It should also be remembered that the shock of discovering that their parents have dementia is still fresh. They are left reeling from this emotional upheaval at the same time that they are being asked to perform myriad tasks for which they have had no preparation. It is little wonder that, shell-shocked over the recent crisis and the assumption of the role, they are unable to unscramble events, perceptions, and motivations in order to determine the path that led them to their present situation.

If one were to ask the question of caregivers in this stage, it might be met with a puzzled look or a nervous giggle. The chuckle might mean that they consider it an absurd question to ask, or it could indicate some slight embarrassment that they are floundering in the role and cannot say how they got there.

The puzzled look might indicate their realization that there may be precipitating factors that led to this state of affairs. It seemed to them to come out of nowhere. They have no answer and do not feel the need for one.

It is a little like an unplanned birth. Yes, there was a triggering event. In this case, it was the onset of dementia. Yet, to ask why one became a caregiver is like asking why one became a parent. There was probably not a thorough discussion with clear, logical, well-thought out reasons for having children. One may be able to point out, in retrospect, some of the positive consequences of producing children—"it strengthened our marriage; they gave us so much joy; they were an outgrowth of our love; there was a desire to form a spiritual union and the children were the tangible results." Most parents, however, would simply respond, "It's just what you do. You get married and have children." For caregivers of parents with dementia, it is much like that: "The crisis occurs and you just do it; you don't ask why."

Where there was no crisis, but rather the triggering events occurred slowly, over time, the caregivers have an equally hard time responding. It is difficult to recall all of the events. There are too many—big and small—to try to add up and make sense of it.

Also in this first phase are caregivers who have actively avoided considering how this happened to them. Some may still be in a form of denial: "I won't think about it. It's not real. And if it is, maybe it's only temporary."

Others do not want to deal with the implications of the question, 'Why me?' To this caregiver it either suggests something negative about her family who has left her to handle this alone, or it implies some flaw in her character for allowing it to happen. Neither of these are propositions that she wants to consider. The question is better left unasked.

Regardless of the reasons, this first stage does not appear to be a time to reflect on the course of events that brought the caregiver to this point in her life. There are times in people's life-journeys when they stop to rest on the metaphorical climb to the top of the mountain. They turn to scan the panorama to see both where they have been and where they are going. The perspective from that vantage point welcomes both retrospection and introspection.

This is not one of those times for the caregiver. At this point in the climb, she is clinging to a narrow ledge by her fingertips. This moment is not about gaining perspective on one's life—it is about survival.

It is not until caregivers are able to gain a more secure perch that they move on to phase two. At this point, caregivers can be divided into two groups. Their grouping reveals something about what they experienced in phase one and a good deal about the direction they will head on their road to self-discovery.

The model presented here will first follow the group on the A-Track through phase five. It will then trace the course taken by those on the B-Track.

Phase Two: Captains of Their Fate

Caregivers in this group seem to have a fairly healthy outlook on life and a positive attitude toward caregiving. Unlike their counterparts from the B-Track, these women believe that they receive some help from their brothers and sisters and other family members and friends. Make no mistake, these daughters are the primary caregivers, handling the bulk of the work, but they do not think that they are alone. They believe that they receive some assistance with caregiving tasks or that they have the financial or emotional support of others.

They have adjusted to the role and have settled into a routine that they feel is do-able. While, at times, they feel that providing care is nearly overwhelming, they still feel in charge. They believe that they were in control at the time that they assumed the role as caregiver, actively choosing the role or willingly accepting it.

Their explanations as to how they came by the role are rather superficial, offered with the cheery air of someone for whom things are going fairly well. Their response is somewhat automatic as when someone asks a person how he is and he responds, "Fine, thanks." The belief is that people are expecting a simple reply. They probably do not want or expect an in-depth analysis, and likely, he has not thought about it enough to give a more complete response.

The responses of these caregivers are likewise immediate, concrete, and simplistic. They answer the question of how they came to the job of caregiver with explanations such as:

Well, I was closest.

I didn't have a family to take care of.

I wasn't really giving up much with the loss of that job.

I was the oldest.

I was better prepared to deal with it.

Most offer these explanations without the hint of resentment. They seem to truly believe that these are the underlying causes of their selection and that they are reason enough.

Others offer these explanations rather half-heartedly, as if, at some level, they are aware that the precipitating factor mentioned should not necessarily lead to the consequence that it did. Still, they, like others in this group, believe themselves to be in a relatively good position, and, thus have no need to explore the question any further.

Caregivers in this group received support, and that made all the difference in their perception of their lot. They have a positive attitude about their role. They feel in charge, and whether or not they actually had any more control in their selection than their counterparts in B-Track, they believe that they did.

Phase Three: The Resolute

In this third stage, caregivers have the advantage of time and some historical perspective to reflect on the situation. No less is demanded of them in terms of care; previous care tasks that are no longer required as the disease progresses are replaced by new ones. However, the women have been in the role long enough at this point to be able to find occasional breathing room for thinking about more than the daily routine.

Women in this group tend to look beyond their initial statement—"I received help." They add to it, "But I'm the one who's carrying the lion's share. I wonder why?"

In this phase they are willing to question, search for underlying truths, and consider complex issues. They are willing to challenge the rather simplistic reasons that they verbalized in the prior phase. Some simply find their earlier statements less satisfying in the light of day that has come with the passing of time. Others probably knew that there were deeper reasons than those that they had previously given; they just were not ready nor had the time to delve into their caregiving past.

They come to see that there is life after caregiving, and their working to understand this role will help them to learn from the experience and be better prepared for future events in their lives. They suspect that some of the factors that influenced their selection may have played a role in other aspects of their lives—other times, other relationships. Understanding this situation will help them to understand their "whole life" better.

They now have the courage to look at the part that they, themselves, played in this decision, beyond the role that parents, siblings, and others may have had in it. It is not an easy task that they have chosen for themselves. They must be willing to expose themselves and their loved ones to closer scrutiny. But they are determined. It is worth some psychic pain to discover real answers in their lives.

Caregivers could remain at this stage of development. Most will continue on to phase four; however, it is possible to skip this phase and advance directly to phase five.

Phase Four: The Revisionists

More than anything else, this seems to be a stage of respite for the caregivers. They have been working hard at gaining an understanding. They have sometimes uncovered truths that have been difficult to accept and deal with. They need a rest from all this soul-searching.

They have dredged up haunting concerns and gained disturbing insights. They feel a need, at this point, for a slight retreat from the vigor of the exploration in phase three. They tend to wrap a protective layer around themselves and their family members. They are reluctant to talk about what they have learned.

They prefer not to talk about feelings that they had or motives which they may have previously attributed to family members. Earlier statements are seen as being disloyal to siblings. There is a backtracking that occurs.

The whole experience begins to be idealized. As they tell the story now, there were good excuses for the failure of others to get involved. They defend their decisions and believe them to be well-thought out and sound.

The actual caregiving experience is described as being less burdensome than would be expected. There is a lighter tone to their speech and demeanor. The role is described in a more positive light, and there is a focus on the rewards of the caregiving experience.

This new perspective could be interpreted as maturation. Just as sixteen year-olds sometimes change their opinions of their parents when they turn twenty-one, maturing in the caregiving role might give daughters a more realistic view of the experience that they have gone through. Somehow, however, it just does not seem to ring true.

Rather, it appears for some caregivers to be a need to make sense of the experience—to give it some meaning, to have it fit into some larger scheme of life. There is a desire to come to terms with some of the issues that have nagged at them. Even if there cannot be complete resolution, they feel a need to put some of the concerns away and get on with life.

There is a need to regain some control over their lives. And while not all may yet be able to do this physically, they can begin the process by redefining the experience in a way that gives them some sense of command of the situation. Regardless of how erratic a path their ship has cut through the turbulent waters of this journey, at least they had a hand on the rudder, and they have some confidence that they can now steer a straighter course.

This phase is as far as most will go. They have given this question all the thought that they are capable of giving. This is the end of their journey. This is likely how they will continue to tell the story and think about the experience for the rest of their lives.

Yet, it is difficult to tell for whom this is a stopping point and for whom it is a resting place—a chance to collect themselves, take respite and recharge for the next phase, probably the most difficult of all. For there is no deadline by which time caregivers must move to the next stage. For some, progress will be rather continuous. In a few short months or years they may progress beyond this point. Others may spend long years at this stopping off point before continuing to phase five. Conceivably, it could take a lifetime.

Phase Five: The Deep-See Divers

For those who reach this phase, there is a conscious decision to return once more to the murky world which they left in phase three. They choose to delve once again into issues that they had left there and covered over in phase four. They have the courage to strip away the veneer of ideality that they had used to hide family blemishes and re-examine the entire experience.

There is an attempt here at real resolution. They are willing to honestly acknowledge and admit shortcomings on the part of their family, friends, society, patients, and themselves. They try to balance, to some extent, the negative side of this experience with the positive—accurately, realistically.

And they reach some level of acceptance with it all. They are able to put the experience in perspective, to integrate it with the whole of life. This is not necessarily a happy phase, but there is some peace achieved.

There are different levels of contentment in this phase. As caregivers and former caregivers move along in this stage, old pains may have been soothed to some extent. Confrontations with family members may have occurred and some resolution found. Regrets are abandoned, as caregivers realize the futility of wasting energy by remaining fixated on that which cannot be changed.

The passing of time is necessary to enter and move along in this phase—much time for most. Yet, time, alone, does not seem to be sufficient for progress. A working relationship with a counselor, clergyman, family member, or close friend may well be a necessary ingredient in the recipe for resolution. Those who have a confidant in whom to confide—someone to listen and help sort through thoughts and feelings—appear to fare better in the activities of this stage than those who attempt it alone.

It also appears that one's personality, intelligence, and insight are major determinants for success in the task of learning how she came to the role of caregiver. Regardless of the passing of time, it is doubtful that everyone will successfully negotiate this phase.

B-Track

While all caregivers begin the task of providing care in phase one with little understanding of their selection for the role, not everyone will continue along the same path of discovery. As caregivers progress beyond this very limited level of understanding, they seem to be divided into two groups: those who received some assistance and support from family and friends, and those who were left to fend for themselves. This latter group proceed down a much different road than their counterparts. Travel on the B-Track tends to be a lonelier journey and typically leads to limited understanding.

Phase Two: The Lone Estrangers

Having received no assistance with the overwhelming burdens of caregiving, women in this group feel alone, alienated, abandoned, and estranged. They believe that there was nobody else to step forward to do the job or, at least, nobody who would. They feel that they really had no choice in the matter.

They were assigned the role of caregiver. Some of these women may have willingly chosen the role had they had the opportunity. Others may have refused it. It is a moot point in their minds, for they believe that they really had no part in the decision.

Many of these women seem unaware of options that may have been available to them. Some of this may be attributable to dualistic thinking. They make statements such as, "Either I take care of her, or she'll go into a nursing home." They think in terms of them taking care of their parents or one of their siblings doing so, but have difficulty thinking of ways to share the responsibility.

Some may actually pass up siblings who would be willing to provide some assistance. There seems to be an inability to know how to ask for help, to solicit support. Time and again women in this group state that there is no one to help. But when asked if they requested assistance, they admit that they have not. The typical explanation is that anyone ought to be able to see that they need help. They do not feel that they should have to ask.

They believe that they are at the mercy of other people and other forces, all outside their control. They make statements such as:

It's fate; you can't fight it.
God chose me to bear this burden.
My dad picked me to take care of Mom.
People say you're supposed to. What are you going to do, say, "No, I won't"?

Many women in this group feel cheated, abused, angry, and resentful, but not all. Some just seem to think, "Oh well, that's fate," and go on with life.

None of these women, however, believe that they are in control of their lives. They have adjusted to the role, but they feel locked in—not just in the role, but in life, in general. One is left with the question, did having this role forced upon them make these women feel out of control, or does their general perception of being out of control of life taint their descriptions of how they became caregivers?

Phase Three: The Resigned

Those in stage three are well-entrenched in their role. They do not even contemplate a time when the role may end. This is the lot that the hand of fate has dealt them; the past, the present and the future are one and the same. If one had no control over her selection, then she has no power to change it, they reason.

They believe that there is no need for exploration of the selection process. What is the sense in it? They are convinced that understanding would change nothing. They are simply resigned to their fate.

They often bitterly accuse their siblings of slacking in their responsibility. They blame them and others for the situation in which they find themselves.

There are some in this group who resist exploration for other reasons, believing that there are those things that are better left alone. Further exploration can do no good and may (if it involves confrontation with painful memories, disturbing thoughts or aggressive siblings) cause harm.

From this point, caregivers can move on to one of two phases. Some will leave the B-Track and move to phase four of the A-Track (The Revisionists, described earlier as idealizing the experience), in a vain attempt to gain some sort of control in their lives. Whether they move to phase four of the A-Track or proceed on to phase four of the B-Track, there is little evidence to suggest that they will progress to phase five.

Phase Four: The Heroines

The daughters in this group take pride in their caregiving burdens. While there is no need to exaggerate, they take great delight in describing their hardships in detail. They relate countless stories of friends, neighbors and family members who have told them, "I just don't know how you do it."

They are at the point where they would probably not accept help if it were offered. They revel in the glory of their martyrdom.

The recognition that they get from the church and community far outweighs the hardships that they must endure. Not only do they get motivation and energy from their position as martyr, but the actual burden of the experience seems to give their lives meaning and significance. It defines a role for them. They believe that they would be lost without it.

While others may see this as a negative role, the suffering daughters may not. Truth be told, they do exhibit an amazing capacity to continue providing care long after most would give up. Some devote hours each day to providing fluids via eyedroppers to vegetative patients. Cynics might suggest that care is continued long after it is in the good of the patient, and raise the question, "Who are you doing this for?"

Postscript to the Theory

It should be understood that this theoretical framework is merely an attempt to organize the information and insights gained from interviewing the fifteen caregiving daughters of the study. It is meant to reflect a structure and process that seemed to emerge as I listened to the taped interviews over and over, and as I replayed our conversations in my mind.

The descriptions of the phases, some of them rather harsh, are not meant to be accusatory or damning. They are not even intended to be critical. They are simply meant to portray an image of what I observed.

I do not mean to imply that any particular caregiver could be, or should be, in any other phase. Assignment to a certain phase or track is not intended as a judgment; it is simply an attempt to categorize for the purpose of elucidation.

Regardless of the phase in which I believe these women to be located, I have the utmost respect for each of them. I truly believe that they are doing the best that they can in understanding their role and in providing care. In the final analysis, not one of these women retreated from the challenge presented to them.

Their reasons for accepting the role vary. Some of these reasons may be viewed by society as more worthy than others. Yet, the honesty and openness of these women have provided a remarkable picture of caregiving that will contribute helpful insights to professionals who work with daughters who provide care. The courage that they displayed in providing those insights should silence those who would make judgments about their worthiness.

POTENTIAL IMPACT OF THE STUDY

Prior to the recognition of dementia as a major disabling condition of the elderly, the lack of research and services left families to their own devices in coping with the devastating effects of mental deterioration. In recent years, much has been learned about the nature of dementia and effective measures for providing care for those who suffer from it. That body of information has enriched the potential knowledge-base and skill-level of all those concerned with patients and their families.

Likewise, the results of this present study have significance for a variety of groups and individuals. Foremost are the daughters who are the caregivers and potential caregivers of parents with dementia. Having an awareness of the processes by which caregivers come to the role could raise one's appreciation for the choices available. A conscious decision to accept or reject the role could replace the daughter's drifting into the role that is so common today.

Those who are already caregivers can benefit, as well. Reviewing the list of thirty-eight factors could help caregivers identify previously unknown reasons for accepting the position. This may lead not only to self-discovery, but to a feeling of connectedness with other caregivers. They might realize that they not only perform similar tasks, but that they do them for similar reasons. This could make them feel less alone—part of something bigger than themselves. It could help to validate their reasons for caring and their feelings about the role. Knowledge of the selection process might help caregivers in their psychological adjustment to the role and could help them become better caregivers.

Making better choices about whether or not to become a caregiver, and feeling better about those choices could have a positive effect on the care that dementia patients receive. Not everyone has the many attributes necessary to provide quality care for persons with dementia. Yet, when no conscious, rational decision is made, one's caregiver could be determined by little more than chance.

This study can have an impact on families, as well. The information coming from the women in the study can help family members better understand the caregiver's feelings and resulting behaviors. They can gain a better understanding of how they can be supportive of the primary caregiver and maintain a sound relationship throughout the course of the disease.

Practitioners from a variety of disciplines—counselors, social workers, clergy, support group leaders, health care providers, and others—can gain a better perspective of who and what they are dealing with when working with a daughter who provides care for a parent with dementia. The study can provide the professional with clues as to the type of assistance that the caregiver may need.

It could also help bring to the attention of policy-makers the plight of adult daughters. With the increase of women in the work force, it may not be possible to continue to rely on them, alone, as the major source of care. The results not only demonstrate the subtle factors that influence the selection of daughters, but also begs the question, "Why not sons?"

The results speak to researchers, too. The methodology used to produce those results made it very clear that the length of time spent with subjects and the amount of time they were given to consider their responses dramatically affected the quantity and quality of the data. This is not an area that lends itself to a question asked as an aside in a broader study. It is also a subject that should be approached cautiously with the use of surveys and questionnaires.

Finally, this research has broad implications for educators from a variety of disciplines. For it is ultimately they who have the responsibility to formally or informally bring this information to the above-mentioned groups.

IMPLICATIONS OF THE FINDINGS

The women in this study had a great deal more to say than they realized at the start. They surprised themselves not only with the amount of information that they had to share, but also with the importance of what they had to say. Often, after they had finished with part of their story, they would appear startled by what they had heard from their own lips, and would say, "Oh, maybe `they' ought to know that."

`They' are other women who these daughters know will one day find themselves in the caregiving role. They felt a kinship to these future caregivers whom they will likely never meet. They wanted to pass on what they had learned, what they were learning. They want to make things easier for the next generation of daughters who provide care.

They never envisioned, however, having anything to say to the professionals who work with caregivers. These women would think that presumptuous. I believe that they have a great deal to say—more than what I was able to hear in the short time that I spent with them. If they were to talk directly to practitioners, this is what I believe they would tell them:

Encourage communication among family members. So many times problems arose, not because of poor communication, but because of no communication. Siblings were left to try to figure out for themselves what the other wanted, needed, or thought. Daughters thought that their brothers and sisters "should know" what they were experiencing. There was little evidence that they did.

Encourage family meetings. Bringing everyone together to discuss options, make joint decisions, and provide emotional support for each other may not always work. However, it has to be more effective than the typical approach of the day, which leaves the caregiver feeling abandoned and the siblings feeling alienated and guilty.

Encourage families to think about the possibility of dementia and make their caregiving wishes known before the need arises. This idea is similar to that of a living will, where individuals make clear, ahead of time, what medical treatments they would choose in the event that they needed medical attention and could no longer make their wishes known. If families could openly explore options for care—including parents in the discussion—at a time when no crisis exists, when there is time to set things in motion, and when emotions are not running high, caregiving decisions would be much improved.

Keep in mind that there are a variety of reasons for giving care. Personalities and life circumstances will vary greatly among caregivers. Do not let your stereotypic image of "the caregiver" lead you to believe, upon first meeting her, that you know who she is or why she provides care. Her reasons are probably complex and almost hopelessly intertwined. The most often stated reasons (or first stated) are not necessarily the most important. Take time to get to know her.

Caregivers appreciate help in understanding their role and how they came to it. Most will need help in this endeavor—someone to listen, to provide feedback. It is not something that is done easily by oneself. Yet, few find anyone willing to provide that kindness.

Understanding of that role is not static. Different reasons for providing care may be more important at one time or another. Caregivers may be at different levels of understanding at different points in time. There is a growth process involved in comprehension of the role. Helping professionals can assist caregivers in gaining increased understanding. Helping to disentangle complex and intertwined issues is an important way to assist them.

Perceptions of caregivers are sometimes narrow, and can be broadened with help. Caregivers sometimes believe that they are the only ones who can provide care for their parents. This is seldom the case, but they may need help in seeing other options. (Help from male members of the family is one option that is often overlooked).

Support for the caregiver means more than physical assistance with activities of care. Emotional support, moral support is every bit as important to most caregivers. For some, it is the most important thing that they could receive from their family. The animosity that caregivers feel toward the siblings whom they believe deserted them most often is a result of what they see as emotional desertion. Family members should understand that they do not have to have the answers to problems; they just have to show that they care by being able to listen.

LIMITATIONS OF THE STUDY

It should be remembered that this is a qualitative study, and as such, no attempt was made to create a representative sample. Neither the small number of 15 subjects nor the method of selection would suggest otherwise. The caregiving daughters who were interviewed were all from West Virginia, and their stories may not be reflective of those from other geographic areas of the country.

The theoretical framework linking the reasons stated by the daughters and the patterns and themes observed by the investigator was developed in retrospect. The interviews had been concluded and the data initially analyzed before any attempt was made to find this underlying structure. Had the theory been conceived prior to the interviews or, at least, formulated as the interviews progressed, there would have been opportunities to ask questions that could have helped confirm the existence of the phases proposed or strengthen the weaker parts of the model.

IMPLICATIONS FOR FURTHER RESEARCH

This investigation was exploratory in nature and, as such, opens the door for a plethora of additional research questions. While this list is not meant to be exhaustive, it identifies those areas that need the most urgent attention.

Most obvious is the question of whether or not there are cultural factors that influence the reasons given by the caregivers. Replication of the study in different geographic regions of the country would shed light on this question.

Having the stories of the 15 daughters, in their own words, is a wonderful source of data. Yet, those stories are not necessarily the actual reasons for their selection as caregiver, but rather their perceptions of how it occurred. It would be interesting to see how the perceptions of other family members compared to those of the women in the study.

Daughters were selected for this study because of their overwhelming prevalence in the caregiving role. Would sons who provide care have the same motivations as daughters?

Most intriguing is the question of daughters being consciously or unconsciously chosen early in life and groomed to position themselves for the role. Does this occur, and, if it does, is it an Appalachian custom? Is the eldest or youngest daughter any more likely than a middle child to assume this role?

The theoretical framework proposed in this paper needs to be tested. Do the phases truly exist? Are there others that did not emerge with the existing data? Are the stages of the model linked to some identifiable factor—stage of the disease, age of the daughter, length of time in the caregiver role? Re-interviewing the same women at two to five year intervals would help in determining whether or not perceptions or levels of understanding truly change over time.

CONCLUSION

In reflection, the caregiving role is seen as bittersweet by most caregivers. It is probably the most difficult and trauma-producing task that they have ever performed. Yet, many say that they have no regrets and would do it again. There are positive as well as negative aspects to the role.

The experience can bring families closer together. This may occur in extended families among siblings, but is more likely to happen within the nuclear family. Spouses and children of primary caregivers can rally around these women, creating a closeness that had not previously existed.

The need created by the mental deterioration of the parent can provide an opportunity for adult daughters to demonstrate their competence. This is especially meaningful for daughters who were unaware of their strengths or who were never acknowledged for strengths that they did possess. Success in the caregiving role can be a source of pride in accomplishing so difficult a task as this.

There is a re-focusing that can occur. Things are put in perspective by the trauma created by dementia. It is difficult to watch the daily struggle of patient and caregiver and not appreciate even the small things in life that are typically taken for granted.

While the virtues of daughters who provide care have been proclaimed throughout this paper, it should not be inferred that there is something wrong with family members who are not primary caregivers. There are good reasons for not taking on the role, and no one needs to defend that decision beyond the boundaries of the family.

It is still surprising how little is known about caregiving. So many decisions are made with so little information. Adult children decide whether or not to assume the role of caregiver with scant knowledge of the processes at work. The decision is seldom based on solid information or logic. Families choose the type of care a loved one will receive with an almost complete lack of information on available options. Government policies are too infrequently based on good research or even personal knowledge and more often made to gain political advantage.

Somehow this must change in the near future. The problem of care of persons with dementia will not go away, but rather continue to grow more complex. The enormous increase in numbers of elderly, the changing roles of women, and the transformation in the structure of the traditional family will only compound the problem. It must be addressed with much more forethought than it is at present.

The first step toward solving a problem is gathering information. The women in this study have provided a good deal of material to be digested. The theoretical framework that has been laid over this information is an attempt to take a complex concept with intertwining issues and organize it in such a way that it can be visualized more clearly for purposes of scrutiny, questioning, discussion and revision. It appears that this research on caregiving daughters does not end with a conclusion, but rather with a starting point.

References

American Psychiatric Association. (1994). *Diagnostic and Statistical Manual of Mental Disorders*, Fourth Edition. Washington, DC: American Psychiatric Association.

Andolsek, K., Clapp-Channing, N., Gehlbach, S., Moore, I., Proffitt, V., Sigmon, S., & Warshaw, G. (1988). Caregivers and elderly relatives: The prevalence of caregiving in a family practice. *Archives of Internal Medicine, 148* (10), 2177-2180.

Ashe, J., Rosen, S., McArthur, J., & Davis L. (1993). Bacterial, fungal, and parasitic causes of dementia. In P. Whitehouse (Ed.), *Dementia* (pp. 276-306). Philadelphia: F.A. Davis.

Baldwin, B. (1990). Family caregiving: Trends and forecasts. *Geriatric Nursing, 11* (4), 172-174.

Barber, C, & Pasley, B. (1995). Family care of Alzheimer's patients: The role of gender and generational relationships on- caregiving outcomes. *Journal of Applied Gerontology,14* (2), 172-192.

Baumgarten, M. (1989). The health of persons giving care to the demented elderly: A critical review of the literature. *Journal of Clinical Epidemiology, 42* (12), 1137-1148.

Benson, D. (1986). Alzheimer's Disease: The pedigree. In A. Scheibel, A. Wechsler, & M. Brazier (Eds.), *The biological substrates of Alzheimer's Disease* (pp. 1-7). Orlando, FL: Academic Press.

Brody, E., Litvin, S., Albert, S., & Hoffman, C. (1994). Marital status of daughters and patterns of care. *Journal of Gerontology, 49* (2), S95-S103.

Brody, E., Litvin, S., Hoffman, C., & Kleban, M. (1995) Marital status of caregiving daughters and co-residence with dependent parents. *The Gerontologist, 35* (1), 75-85.

Brody, E., & Schoonover, C. (1986). Patterns of parent-care when adult daughters work and when they do not. *The Gerontologist, 26,* 372-381.

Butler, R. (1990). Senile dementia of the Alzheimer's type (SDAT). In W. Abrams & R. Berkow (Eds.), *The Merck Manual of Geriatrics* (pp. 933-938). Rathway, NJ: Merck Sharp and Dohme Research Laboratories.

Cantor, M., & Hirshorn, B. (1989). Intergenerational transfers within the family context—motivating factors and their implication for caregiving. *Women and Health, 14* (3/4), 39-51.

Caserta, M., Lund, D., Wright, S., & Redburn, D. (1987). Caregivers to dementia patients: The utilization of community services. *The Gerontologist, 27* (2), 209-214.

Choi, H. (1993) Cultural and noncultural factors as determinants of caregiver burden for the impaired elderly in South Korea. *The Gerontologist, 33* (1), 8-15.

Cicirelli, V. (1981). *Helping elderly parents: The role of adult children.* Boston, MA: Auburn House.

Civil, R., Whitehouse, P., Lanska, D., & Mayeux, R. (1993). Degenerative dementias. In P. Whitehouse (Ed.), *Dementia* (pp. 167-214). Philadelphia: F.A. Davis.

Clark, M. (1984, December). A slow death of the mind. *Newsweek,* pp. 56-62.

Corcoran, M. (1992). Gender differences in dementia management plans of spousal caregivers: Implications for occupational therapy. *American Journal of Occupational Therapy, 46* (11), 1006-1012.

Coyne, A., Reichman, W., & Berbig, L. (1993). The relationship between dementia and elder abuse. *The American Journal of Psychiatry, 150* (4), 643-646.

Cummings, J., & Benson, D. (1983). *Dementia: A clinical approach.* Boston: Butterworths.

Dhooper, S. (1992). Caregivers of Alzheimer's Disease patients: A review of the literature. *Journal of Gerontological Social Work, 18* (1-2), 19-37.

Dwyer, J. W., & Coward, R. T. (1991). A multivariate comparison of the involvement of adult sons versus daughters in the care of impaired parents. *Journal of Gerontology, 46* (5), S259-269.

Eckert, J., & Shulman, S. (1996). Daughters caring for their aging mothers: A mid-life developmental process. *Journal of Gerontological Social Work. 25* (3-4), 17-32.

Edwards, A. (1993). *Dementia.* New York: Plenum.

Emery, V. (1992). Interaction of language and memory in major depression and senile dementia of the Alzheimer's type. In L. Backman (Ed.),

Memory functioning in dementia (pp. 175-204). Amsterdam: Elsevier Science Publishers.

Feldman, E., & Plum, F. (1993). Metabolic dementia. In P. Whitehouse (Ed.), *Dementia* (pp. 307-336). Philadelphia: F.A. Davis.

Finley, N. J., Roberts, M. D., & Banahan, B.F. (1988). Motivators and inhibitors of attitudes of filial obligation toward aging parents. *The Gerontologist, 28*, 73-78.

Fradkin, L., & Heath, A. (1992). *Caregiving of older adults*. Santa Barbara, CA: ABC-CLIO.

Franks, M. M., & Stephens, M. A. (1992). Multiple roles of middle-generation caregivers: Contextual effects and psychological mechanisms. *Journal of Gerontology, 47* (3), S123-129.

Fraser, M. (1987). *Dementia: It nature and management*. Avon, Great Britain: Bath Press.

Gellatly, J. (1987). Supporting the Alzheimer's caregiver. In K. O'Connor & J. Prothero (Eds.), *The Alzheimer's Caregiver: Strategies for support* (pp. 67-83). Seattle: University of Washington Press.

George, L. K., & Gwyther, L. P. (1986). Caregiver well-being: A multidimensional examination of family caregivers of demented adults. *The Gerontologist, 26* (3), 253-259.

Greenberg, J. S., Boyd, M. D., & Hale, J. F. (1992). *The caregiver's guide: For caregivers and the elderly*. Chicago: Nelson-Hall.

Greene, V. L., & Monahan, D. J. (1989). The effect of a support and education program on stress and burden among family caregivers to frail elderly persons. *The Gerontologist, 29* (4), 472-477.

Group for the Advancement of Psychiatry. (1988). *The psychiatric treatment of Alzheimer's Disease*. New York: Brummer/Mazel.

Guberman, N., Maheu, P., & Maille, C. (1992). Women as family caregivers: Why do they care? *The Gerontologist, 32*, 607-617.

Gwyther, L. P. (1985). *Care of Alzheimer's patients: A manual for nursing home staff*. American Health Care Association and ADRDA.

Hardy, V. L., & Riffle, K. L. (1993). Support for caregivers of dependent elderly: A support group can help a dependent elderly person by helping a caregiver overcome feelings of social isolation. *Geriatric Nursing 14* (3), 161-164.

Henderson, J. N., Gutierrez-Mayka, M., Garcia, J., & Boyd, S. (1993). A model for Alzheimer's Disease support group development in African-American and Hispanic populations. *The Gerontologist 33* (3), 409-414.

Heston, L., & White, J. (1983). *Dementia: A practical guide to Alzheimer's Disease and related illnesses*. New York: W. H. Freeman.

Himes, C. (1994). Parental caregiving by adult women. *Research on Aging, 16* (2), 191-211.

Himes, C, Jordan, A., & Farkas, J. (1996). Factors influencing parental caregiving by adult women. *Research on Aging, 18* (3), 349-370.

Hooyman, N., & Lustbader, W. (1986). *Taking care: Supporting older people and their families.* New York: Free Press.

Horowitz, A. (1985). Sons and daughters as caregivers to older parents: Differences in role performance and consequences. *The Gerontologist, 25,* 612-617.

Ingersoll-Dayton, B., Starrels, M., & Dowler, D. (1996). Caregiving for parents and parents-in-law: Is gender important? *The Gerontologist, 36* (4), 483-491.

Kobayashi, S., Masaki, H., & Noguchi, M. (1993). Developmental process: Family caregivers of demented Japanese. *Journal of Gerontological Nursing, 19* (10), 7-12.

Koo, E., & Price, D. (1993). Neurobiology of dementia. In P. Whitehouse (Ed.), *Dementia* (pp. 55-91). Philadelphia: F. A. Davis.

Kuhlman, G. J., Wilson, H. S., Hutchinson, S. A., & Wallhagen, M. (1991). Alzheimer's Disease and family caregiving: Critical synthesis of the literature and research agenda. *Nursing Research, 40* (6), 331-337.

Lampe, T. (1987). The nature of Alzheimer's Disease: Scientific perspectives. In K. O'Connor, & J. Prothero (Eds.), *The Alzheimer's caregiver: Strategies for support* (pp. 3-21). Seattle: University of Washington Press.

Lanska, D., & Schoenberg, B. (1993). Epidemiology of dementia: Methodologic issues and approaches. In P. Whitehouse (Ed.), *Dementia* (pp. 3-33). Philadelphia: F. A. Davis.

Lawton, M., Kleban, M., Moss, M., Rovine, M., & Glicksman, A. (1989). Measuring caregiving appraisal. *Journal of Gerontology, 44,* 61.

Lieberman, M. A., & Kramer, J. H. (1991). Factors affecting decisions to institutionalize demented elderly. *The Gerontologist, 31* (3), 371-374.

Mace, N., & Rabins, P. (1991). *The 36-hour day* (rev. ed.). Baltimore: The Johns Hopkins University Press.

Mace, N., Whitehouse, P., & Smyth, K. (1993). Management of patients with dementia. In P. Whitehouse (Ed.), *Dementia* (pp. 400-416). Philadelphia: F. A. Davis.

Maletta, G. (1990). The concept of "reversible" dementia: How nonreliable terminology may impair effective treatment. *Journal of the American Geriatric Society, 38* (2), 136-140.

Maletta, G., & Hepburn, K. (1986). Helping families cope with Alzheimer's: The physician's role. *Geriatrics, 41* (11), 81-84.

Malonebeach, E. E., & Zarit, S. H. (1991). Current research issues in caregiving to the elderly. *International Journal of Aging and Human Development, 32* (2), 103-114.

Marks, N. (1996). Caregiving across the lifespan: National prevalence and predictors. *Family Relations, 45*, 27- 36.

Marshall, J. (1993). Vascular dementias. In P. Whitehouse (Ed.), *Dementia* (pp. 215-236). Philadelphia: F. A. Davis.

Matthews, S. (1995). Gender and the division of filial responsibility between lone sisters and their brothers. *Journal of Gerontology, 50B* (5), S312-S320.

Matthews, S. H., & Rossner, T. T. (1988). Shared filial responsibility: The family as the primary caregiver. *Marriage and Family Living, 50*, 185-195.

McArthur, J., Roos, R., & Johnson, R. (1993). Viral dementias. In P. Whitehouse (Ed.), *Dementia* (pp. 237-275). Philadelphia: F. A. Davis.

Merrill, D. (1993). Daughters-in-law as caregivers to the elderly. *Research on Aging, 15* (1), 70-91.

Miller, B., & Cafasso, L. (1992). Gender differences in caregiving: Fact or artifact? *The Gerontologist, 32* (4), 498-507.

Miller, B., & Furner, S. (1994). Change in the number of informal helpers of frail older persons. *Public Health Reports, 109* (4), 583-586.

Miller, B., & Montgomery, A. (1990). Family caregivers and limitations in social activities. *Research on Aging, 12* (1), 72-93.

Miller, D. B., Gulle, N., & McCue, F. (1986). Realities of respite for families, clients, and sponsors. *The Gerontologist, 26* (5), 467-470.

Morse, J. M. (1989). *Qualitative nursing research: A contemporary dialogue.* Rockville, MD: Aspen.

Motenko, A. K. (1989). The frustrations, gratifications, and well-being of dementia caregivers. *The Gerontologist, 29* (2), 166-172.

Mui, A. C. (1992). Caregiver strain among black and white daughter caregivers: A role theory perspective. *The Gerontologist, 32* (2), 203-212.

Mui, A. C. (1995). Caring for frail elderly parents: A comparison of adult sons and daughters. *The Gerontologist, 35* (1), 86-93.

National Institutes of Health. (1995). *Alzheimer's Disease: Unraveling the mystery* (NIH Publication No. 95-3782). Washington, DC: U.S. Government Printing Office.

Novak, M., & Guest, C. (1989). Caregiver response to Alzheimer's Disease. *International Journal of Aging and Human Development, 28* (1), 67-79.

Parks, S. H., & Pilisuk, M. (1991). Caregiver burden: gender and psychological costs of caregiving. *American Journal of Orthopsychiatry, 61* (4), 501-509.

Penrod, J., Kane, R. A., Kane, R. L., & Finch, M. D. (1995). Who cares? The size, scope, and composition of the caregiver support system. *The Gerontologist, 35* (4), 489-497.

Pett, M. A., Caserta, M. S., Hutton, A. P., Lund, D. A. (1988). Intergenerational conflict: Middle-aged women caring for demented older relatives. *American Journal of Orthopsychiatry, 58* (3), 405-417.

Powell, L., & Courtice, K. (Eds.). (1986). *Alzheimer's Disease: A guide for families.* Reading, MA: Addison- Wesley.

Pratt, C., Schmall, V., & Wright, S. (1987). Ethical concerns of family caregivers to dementia patients. *The Gerontologist, 27* (5), 632-638.

Pruchno, R. A., Michaels, J. E., & Potashnik, S. L. (1990). Predictors of institutionalization among Alzheimer's Disease victims with caregiving spouses. *Journal of Gerontology, 45* (6), S259-266.

Quayhagen, M. P., & Quayhagen, M. (1988). Alzheimer's stress: Coping with the caregiving role. *The Gerontologist, 28* (3), 391-396.

Reisberg, B. (1986). *Alzheimer's Disease: A clinical update* [Videotape]. Secaucus, NJ: Network For Continuing Medical Education.

Robinson, B. (1983). Validation of a caregiver strain index. *Journal of Gerontology, 38*, 344-348.

Robinson, K. M. (1988). Social skills training program for adult caregivers. *Advances in Nursing Science, 10* (2), 59-72.

Robison, J., Moen, P., & Dempster-McClain, D. (1995). Women's caregiving: Changing profiles and pathways. *Journal of Gerontology, 50B* (6), S362-S373.

Sawyer, J., Ballard, E., & Autrey, P. (1990). *Caring for the memory impaired: Strategies and techniques that work* (rev. ed.). Raleigh, NC: North Carolina Department of Human Resources.

Schmidt, G. L., & Keyes, B. (1985). Group psychotherapy with family caregivers of demented patients. *The Gerontologist, 25* (4), 347-350.

Selig, S., Tomlinson, T., & Hickey, T. (1991). Ethical dimensions of intergenerational reciprocity: Implications for practice. *The Gerontologist, 31* (5), 624-630.

Shanas, E., & Streib, G. (Eds.). (1965). *Social structure and the family: Generational relations.* Englewood Cliffs, NJ: Prentice-Hall.

Sisson, P., & Gilbreath, P. (1987). Families and the fragmented service delivery system. In K. O'Connor, & J. Prothero (Eds.), *The Alzheimer's caregiver* (pp. 84-94). Seattle: University of Washington Press.

Sorensen, S., & Zarit, S. H. (1996). Preparation for caregiving: A study of multigeneration families. *International Journal of aging and Human Development,* 42 (1), 43-63.

Springer, D., & Brubaker, T. H. (1984). *Family caregivers and dependent elderly: Minimizing stress and maximizing independence.* Beverly Hills, CA: Sage.

Steinmetz, S. (1988). *Duty bound: Elder abuse and family care.* Newbury Park, CA: Sage Publications.

Stoller, E. D. (1985). Parental caregiving by adult children. *Journal of Marriage and the Family, 45,* 851-857.

Stone, R., Cafferata, G. L., & Sangl, J. (1987). Caregivers of the frail elderly: A national profile. *The Gerontologist, 27* (5), 616-626.

Stone, R. I., & Short, P. F. (1990). The competing demands of employment and informal caregiving to disabled elders. *Medical Care, 28* (6), 513-526.

Teunisse, S., Derix, M. M., & van Crevel, H. (1991). Assessing the severity of dementia: Patient and caregiver. *Archives of Neurology, 48* (3), 274-277.

Torack, R. (1981). *Your brain is younger than you think: A guide to mental aging.* Chicago: Nelson-Hall. Toseland, R. W., & Rossiter, C. M. (1989). Group interventions to support family caregivers: A review and analysis. *The Gerontologist, 29* (4), 438-448.

U. S. Department of Health and Human Services. (1984). *Alzheimer's Disease: A scientific guide for health practitioners.* Bethesda, MD: National Institutes of Health.

Vitaliano, P. P., Russo, J., Young, H. M., Becker, J., & Maiuro, R. D. (1991). The screen for caregiver burden. *The Gerontologist, 31* (1), 76-83.

Vitaliano, P. P., Russo, J., Young, H. M., Teri, L., & Maiuro, R. D. (1991). Predictors of burden in spouse caregivers of individuals with Alzheimer's Disease. *Psychology and Aging, 6* (3), 392-402.

Wang, H. (1977). Dementia of old age. In W. Smith & M. Kinsbourne (Eds.), *Aging and dementia* (pp. 1-24). New York: Spectrum Publications.

Whitehouse, P. (Ed.). (1993). *Dementia.* Philadelphia: F. A. Davis.

Williamson, G. M., & Schulz, R. (1990). Relationship orientation, quality of prior relationship, and distress among caregivers of Alzheimer's patients. *Psychology and Aging, 5* (4), 502-509.

Wood, F. G. (1991). The meaning of caregiving. *Rehabilitation Nursing, 16* (4), 195-198.

Wright, L. K. (1991). The impact of Alzheimer's Disease on the marital relationship. *The Gerontologist, 31* (2), 224-237.

Yaffe, M. J. (1988). Implications of caring for an aging parent. *Canadian Medical Association Journal, 138* (3). 231-235.

Zarit, S., Orr, N., & Zarit, J. (1985). *The hidden victims of Alzheimer's Disease: Families under stress*. New York: New York University Press.

Zarit, S., Reeves, K., & Bach-Peterson, J. (1980). Relatives of the impaired elderly: Correlates of feelings of burden. *The Gerontologist, 20,* 649-655.

Appendix A

Caregivers
Percent by Gender

**Men
28%**

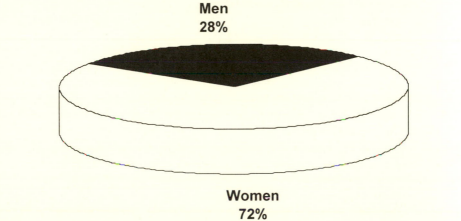

**Women
72%**

Original source: Select Committee on Aging

Caregivers
Percent by Relationship

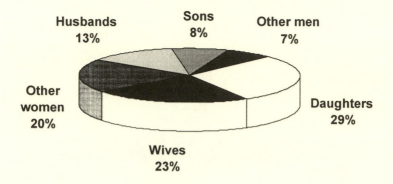

Original source: Select Committee on Aging

Appendix B

DEMOGRAPHICS

1. Code—

2. DOB—

3. Relationship of patient—

4. Age of patient—

5. Dates of care—

6. # of siblings—

7. Marital status of patient—

8. Marital status of caregiver—

9. Ages of caregiver's children—

10. Health status of caregiver—

11. Employment status of caregiver—

12. Birth rank of caregiver—

13. Eventual diagnosis of patient—

Above information pertains to the beginning of the caregiving relationship unless otherwise specified.

AGE OF SUBJECT AT TIME OF INTERVIEW

Subject	Age
Amelia	56
Bernice	45
Callie	64
Dorothy	55
Evelyn	50
Flora	59
Georgia	49
Helen	60
Isabel	66
Jackie	48
Kathleen	52
Laura	42
Maureen	64
Nellie	53
Opal	77

Mean: 56

Range: 42-77

AGE OF SUBJECT AT START OF CAREGIVING

Subject	Age
Amelia	44
Bernice	37
Callie	47
Dorothy	36
Evelyn	39
Flora	53
Georgia	41
Helen	54
Isabel	58
Jackie	48
Kathleen	45
Laura	38
Maureen	53
Nellie	50
Opal	69

Mean: 47.5

Range: 36-69

LENGTH OF CARE BY FAMILY CAREGIVER

Subject	Years of Care
Amelia	6
Bernice	9
Callie	17
Dorothy	11
Evelyn	10
Flora	4
Georgia	6
Helen	6
Isabel	8
Jackie	1/2
Kathleen	7
Laura	4
Maureen	2
Nellie	3
Opal	8

Mean: 6.75

Range: 1/2—17

SIBLINGS OF SUBJECT (FAMILY CAREGIVER)

Subject	Brothers	Sisters	Siblings
Amelia	1	2	3
Bernice	2	0	2
Callie	1	1	2
Dorothy	2	3	5
Evelyn	0	0	0
Flora	0	0	0
Georgia	1	2	3
Helen	0	1	1
Isabel	4	2	6
Jackie	1	1	2
Kathleen	4	1	5
Laura	2	4	6
Maureen	1	2	3
Nellie	3	0	3
Opal	0	1	1

Mean # of Siblings: 3

Range: 0-6

MARITAL STATUS OF PATIENT AT START OF CAREGIVING

Patient	Status
Amelia	M
Bernice	W
Callie	W
Dorothy	W
Evelyn	W
Flora	W
Georgia	W (Twice)
Helen	W
Isabel	M
Jackie	W
Kathleen	W
Laura	M
Maureen	W
Nellie	W
Opal	W

Total Married: 3
Total Widowed: 12
Total Divorced: 0
Total Single: 0

MARITAL STATUS OF SUBJECT AT START OF CAREGIVING

Subject	Status
Amelia	M
Bernice	M
Callie	M
Dorothy	M
Evelyn	D
Flora	M
Georgia	S
Helen	D
Isabel	M
Jackie	D
Kathleen	D
Laura	D
Maureen	W
Nellie	D
Opal	M

Total Married: 7
Total Widowed: 1
Total Divorced: 6
Total Single: 1

CHILDREN OF SUBJECTS (FAMILY CAREGIVERS)

Subject	Daughters	Sons	Children
Amelia	1	3	4
Bernice	0	1	1
Callie	2	1	3
Dorothy	1	0	1
Evelyn	0	0	0
Flora	1	0	1
Georgia	0	0	0
Helen	3	1	4
Isabel	2	2	4
Jackie	3	1	4
Kathleen	1	1	2
Laura	0	2	2
Maureen	1	0	1
Nellie	1	0	1
Opal	2	1	3

Mean Number of Daughters: 1.2 Range: 0-3
Mean Number of Sons: .9 Range: 0-3
Mean Number of Children: 2 Range: 0-4

AGES OF CHILDREN OF SUBJECTS AT START OF
CAREGIVING

Subject	Ages of Daughters	Ages of Sons
Amelia	19	22, 16, 14
Bernice	—	16
Callie	27, 15	22
Dorothy	10	—
Evelyn	—	—
Flora	31	—
Georgia	—	—
Helen	36, 35, 23	18
Isabel	39, 28	37, 31
Jackie	21	25
Laura	—	16, 6
Maureen	29	—
Nellie	21	—
Opal	42, 35	46

Mean Age of Daughters: 26 Range: 10-42
Mean Age of Sons: 23 Range: 6-46
Mean Age of Children: 24.5 Range: 6-46

REPORTED HEALTH OF SUBJECTS AT START OF CAREGIVING

Subject	Reported Health
Amelia	Good
Bernice	Good
Callie	Good
Dorothy	Good
Evelyn	Good
Flora	Good
Georgia	Has C.P., Hyperthyroid
Helen	Fair (Takes nerve pill)
Isabel	Good, Hypertension
Jackie	Good
Kathleen	Good
Laura	Good
Maureen	Good
Nellie	Fair
Opal	Good

Number in Excellent Health: 0
Number in Good Health: 12
Number in Fair Health: 1
Number in Poor Health: 1

EMPLOYMENT STATUS OF SUBJECTS
AT START OF CAREGIVING

Subject	Employment Status
Amelia	Employed
Bernice	Employed
Callie	Not Employed
Dorothy	Part-time
Evelyn	Employed
Flora	Part-time
Georgia	Not Employed
Helen	Employed
Isabel	Employed
Jackie	Employed
Kathleen	Employed
Laura	Employed
Maureen	Not Employed
Nellie	Not Employed
Opal	Retired

Number Employed Outside the Home: 10
Number Not Employed Outside the Home: 5

BIRTH RANK OF SUBJECTS
(FAMILY CAREGIVER)

Subject	Birth Rank
Amelia	Youngest
Bernice	Youngest
Callie	Eldest
Dorothy	Next to Youngest
Evelyn	Only Child
Flora	Only Child
Georgia	Youngest
Helen	Youngest
Isabel	Eldest
Jackie	Eldest
Kathleen	Next to Eldest
Laura	5th Eldest
Maureen	Middle
Nellie	2nd Youngest
Opal	Eldest

Number of Eldest: 4
Number of Youngest: 4
Number of Only Children: 2
Number of Middle Children: 5
Number of Eldest and Youngest (including only): 10

EVENTUAL DIAGNOSIS OF PATIENT

Patient	Diagnosis
Amelia	Alzheimer's & Parkinson's
Bernice	Alzheimer's
Callie	Alzheimer's
Dorothy	Alzheimer's
Evelyn	Dementia
Flora	Dementia
Georgia	Alzheimer's
Helen	Huntington's, Dementia
Isabel	Dementia
Jackie	Alzheimer's
Kathleen	Alzheimer's
Laura	Dementia
Maureen	Alzheimer's
Nellie	Stroke, Senile Dementia
Opal	Dementia

Total Number of Alzheimer's Disease: 8
Total Number of Other Dementias: 7

RESIDENCE OF SUBJECTS
AT TIME OF INTERVIEW

Subject	*Town/City Over 25,000*
Amelia	Yes
Bernice	No
Callie	Yes
Dorothy	Yes
Evelyn	Yes
Flora	No
Georgia	Yes
Helen	No
Isabel	No
Jackie	Yes
Kathleen	Yes
Laura	No
Maureen	No
Nellie	No
Opal	Yes

Number Residing in Town/City over 25,000: 8
Number Residing in Town/City under 25, 000: 7

YEARS ELAPSED SINCE
SUBJECT WAS A PRIMARY CAREGIVER

Subject	Years Elapsed
Amelia	6
Bernice	Still Caring
Callie	1
Dorothy	8
Evelyn	2
Flora	2
Georgia	3
Helen	Still Caring
Isabel	3 Months
Jackie	Still Caring
Kathleen	Still Caring
Laura	Still Caring
Maureen	9
Nellie	Still Caring
Opal	2 Weeks

Range: 0-8

RACE OF SUBJECT

Subject	Race
Amelia	Caucasian
Bernice	Caucasian
Callie	Caucasian
Dorothy	Caucasian
Evelyn	Caucasian
Flora	Caucasian
Georgia	Caucasian
Helen	Caucasian
Isabel	Caucasian
Jackie	African-American
Kathleen	African-American
Laura	Caucasian
Maureen	Caucasian
Nellie	Caucasian
Opal	Caucasian

Total Number Caucasian—13
Total Number African-American—2

SEX OF PATIENT

Patient	Sex
Amelia	F
Bernice	F
Callie	F
Dorothy	F
Evelyn	F
Flora	F
Georgia	F
Helen	F
Isabel	F
Jackie	F
Kathleen	F
Laura	F
Maureen	M
Nellie	F
Opal	F

AGE OF PATIENT
AT START OF CAREGIVING

Subject	Age
Amelia	81
Bernice	76
Callie	65
Dorothy	73
Evelyn	65
Flora	81
Georgia	63
Helen	59
Isabel	76
Jackie	75
Kathleen	58
Laura	75
Maureen	79
Nellie	75
Opal	87

Mean: 72.5

Range: 58-87

Appendix C

NUMBER OF DIFFERENT FACTORS GIVEN BY EACH CAREGIVER

Amelia.. 10
Bernice.. 15
Callie.. 8
Dorothy.. 18
Evelyn.. 10
Flora... 10
Georgia 11
Helen.. 11
Isabel.. 8
Jackie 14
Kathleen 6
Laura.. 13
Maureen 8
Nellie.. 13
Opal.. 11

Range: 6-18
Mean: 11.66

FACTORS LISTED BY CATEGORY
(Number of Times Each Was Given)

Logistical Factors (28)
    Proximity—9
    No one else available—13
    Helping parents remain in their own homes—6
Socialization Factors (23)
    Duty to take care of others—4
    Responsibility to parents—9
    Responsibility of eldest child—1
    Obligation to care—6
    Woman's role—1
    Lesson for the next generation—2
Personality Factors (17)
    Emotional strength—4
    Compassion—3
    Nurturance—2
    Take charge personality—3
    Patience—1
    Cannot say `no'—4
Parent-Child Relationship Factors (26)
    Closeness of relationship—10
    Love—6
    Relationship with non-demented parent—1
    Continuation of earlier role—
Factor Healing Psychic Wounds (6)
    Avoiding feelings of guilt—3
    Resolving poor relationship from the past—2
    Seeking parent's love—1
Exchange Factors (12)
    Reciprocity—10
    Beyond reciprocity—2
Factors Relating to Quality of Care (15)
    Avoiding placement in a nursing home—8
    Daughter's belief that she can provide best care—7

Factors Relating to Sibling Relationships (16)
> Family just assumed that she would be the caregiver—3
> Easier to assume role than to fight with sibling—1
> Avoiding guilt of asking sibling for help—3
> Belief that none of her siblings would provide care—9

External Locus of Control Factors (21)
> Patient decided—3
> Another family member decided—4
> Role evolved slowly over time—7
> Natural, normal part of the life cycle—2
> Religious reasons—4
> An accident, purely chance—1

Factors That Benefit the Caregiver (2)
> Financial incentive—1
> Recognition—1

Index